GETTING HIRED

GETTING HIRED

∽

How to prepare to compete
and win the job you want
now and in the future

By Paul McBlaine

— LPM Press —

Copyright

Copyright © 2020 Paul McBlaine

All rights reserved. No part of this publication may be reproduced, distributed, or transmitted in any form or by any means, including photocopying, recording, or other electronic or mechanical methods, without the prior written permission of the publisher, except in the case of brief quotations embodied in critical reviews and certain other noncommercial uses permitted by copyright law.

ISBN: 978-1-7357668-0-5 (Paperback)
ISBN: 978-1-7357668-1-2 (ebook)
Library of Congress Control Number: 2020919155

Front cover image by Mikk Tonissoo
Book design by Paul McBlaine

Printed in the United States of America

First printing edition 2020

LPM Press
www.LPMPress.com

For information contact:
editor@lpmpress.com

Dedication

I dedicate this book to my lovely wife, Lili, and darling daughter Mahsa, who have suffered with me to birth this project. They reviewed innumerable drafts and provided candid and sometimes brutal commentary that drove me to improve each new draft. They both were, and continue to be, enormously patient.

Table of Contents

A Note to the Reader	ix
PHASE 1 - INVESTIGATE	
Begin at the Beginning	3
Making the Most of Your Experience	9
Coping with Stress	15
Identifying Your Career Options	25
Learn About the Job Market	31
PHASE 2 - FOCUS	
How to Choose a Career	37
Selecting Your Career	43
Become an Expert in Your Selected Career	47
PHASE 3 - PREPARE	
Create a Personal Marketing Message	53
Getting Your Resume to the Right Person	59
Create a Winning Resume	65
Just-in-Time Cover Letters	73
Create a Winning LinkedIn Profile	81
PHASE 4 - LAUNCH	
Plan Your Job Search Campaign	89
Accelerate Your Networking	93
Mining Your Network	101
Launch Your Campaign	109
Working with Recruiters and Headhunters	115
PHASE 5 - WIN	
Crush Your Job Interviews	123
After Your Interview	137
After You Are Hired	143
Parting Advice and Final Words	145
RESOURCES	
Thoughts and Suggestions from Colleagues	151
Online Resources	163
Your First Hundred Days Checklist	164

A NOTE TO THE READER

Without labor, nothing prospers. - Sophocles

Your career is your most important job. Unless you are an entrepreneur or independently wealthy, you will spend a considerable amount of time looking for employment throughout your career. Even if you want a different job in your current company, you need to be prepared to apply and interview for your new position. If you are well prepared, you will get the job you want. Make no mistake, getting hired is a competition. This book will help you discover what you want and learn how to ask for it, compete and win..

Perhaps you already have a job, but you are not happy in your current position; you might want a promotion, be out of work, or have just graduated. Further, you may not yet know what job you can do, what career will make you happy, or how you want to pivot your career. There is an infinite number of reasons why you might look for something new, but to make a career change, you need to get hired.

At some point in everyone's career, they will need to change jobs, careers, or both. Even the CEO of a company will eventually need to find another position, maybe a board position, or become a CEO at a different company. Nothing lasts forever, and you need to prepare for the change.

There is, and will continue to be, enormous competition for jobs at all levels. You are not alone. There are millions of people in your position searching for a job, and millions of jobs available. Yet, there are still hundreds of thousands of open opportunities that go unfilled. Well-qualified individuals are unable to secure a job. Many people won't even get a response to an application or a simple screening interview.

Why? Because, they lack focus, are not prepared, and not going about their job search campaign in the best way. They don't stand out from the crowd, and to be successful, you must stand out!

Your challenge is to compete and win. I created the Getting Hired Program to help my clients stand above their competition. The Program helps them be more confident by showing them how to conduct thorough research and job search preparation.

There are generally two ways of finding a job: networking or applying to a job posting. The Getting Hired Program is a step-by-step guide to successfully managing careers using both approaches. Adequate preparation demonstrates to any employer that the candidate cared enough to do their homework. The rest of the decision comes down to personality. Well-prepared candidates will be able to confidently present their character in the best light and get hired.

The book guides you on how to complete each phase. With the Getting Hired Program, you will be better equipped, more knowledgeable, and better prepared to compete and WIN!

A NOTE TO THE READER

The Getting Hired Program

The five phases of the Getting Hired Program address knowing your options, making a choice, getting focused, creating your marketing materials, launching a job search campaign, and getting hired.

PHASE 1: INVESTIGATE - Building Knowledge

You will learn more about yourself, including personal career wants, your career stage, and the capabilities, skills, and unique traits that make you successful. Learn how to achieve background knowledge about different careers, jobs, and industries. Learn the importance of career pivoting in reaching your dream destination. Use your knowledge to create a list of options

PHASE 2: FOCUS - Making a Meaningful Decision

You will identify your career options and create a systematic way of ranking them in order of priority and narrowing your options to help you choose a career path. You will focus your efforts on one or two career options.

PHASE 3: PREPARE - Developing a Personal Marketing Package

You will develop practical tools to promote yourself, such as a compelling LinkedIn profile, a winning resume, and outstanding cover letters that incorporate personal backstories and a powerful personal marketing message.

PHASE 4: LAUNCH - Launching a Job Search Campaign

You will plan your job search campaign by focusing on networking and on-line job applications. You will expand and get the most out of your network, and you will create SMART goals and track your progress.

PHASE 5: WIN - Getting Hired

You will learn how to crush your job interviews, respond to offers, and kick off your new job using a comprehensive "First Hundred Days Checklist."

THE GETTING HIRED PROGRAM

PHASE 1 - INVESTIGATE

BUILDING KNOWLEDGE

Chapter One

BEGIN AT THE BEGINNING

You have to do the research. If you don't know about something, you have to ask the right people who do. - Spike Lee

To do anything well, you must be fully prepared to succeed and overcome the challenges you might face. If you are better prepared than your competition, you will have a better chance of getting hired. Education and experience are the foundations of being prepared, but you need to continue learning and do detailed research to be competitive.

I chose **INVESTIGATION - BUILDING KNOWLEDGE** as Phase One because I believe in sharpening the saw before you start cutting. You will find greater success if you do extensive research before developing and refining your marketing materials, and well before launching your job search.

WHAT IS A CAREER

The Merriam-Webster Dictionary defines the word career as: *"a field for or pursuit of consecutive progressive achievement, especially in public, professional, or business life."*

Your career is how you spend your time working. You work in jobs, and at companies within industries. All of your work experiences make up your career.

Your career path is like running a race. A runner's goal may be to simply complete the race, or at advanced levels, win. But a runner knows that dreams does not assure success. You sign up, show up, and then, *"Ready, Set, Go!"* You will get started, but will you finish? Will you meet your goal? Without proper preparation and training, the answer is NO!

GETTING HIRED

Preparation is what gives a runner any hope of meeting their goal, and the same goes for finding a job that matches your career objectives. Hence, proper preparation is critical. If you short-cut your preparation, you will suffer and fail like the untrained runner. Prepare well, and you will get your job.

CAREER STAGES

Your career will not be a straight line from point A to point B. You may need to go sideways to go forward. You may take an unexpected opportunity when presented to you, even though the job is somewhat off the trail. To be continuously successful, you must be agile and prepared for a change at all stages of your career. The career stage is determined by what you want your next step to be. The three general stages, with examples are:

1. LATERAL MOVE

You are looking for the same level position in a different company within the same industry.

- Example: Manager of IT at General Car Co. looking for a position as Manager of IT at Worldwide Car Co.

2. PROMOTION

You are looking for a promotion in the same or different company within the same industry.

- Example: Manager of IT at General Car Co. looking for Director of IT at General Car Company
- Example: Manager of IT at General Car Co. looking for Director of IT at Worldwide Car Co.

3. PIVOT

You are looking at a different or new career path at any level in the same or different company in the same or different industry.

BEGIN AT THE BEGINNING

- Example: Recent university graduates seeking their first full-time position.
- Example: Manager of IT at General Car Co. seeking an entry-level position in the supply chain at General Car Co.
- Example: Manager of IT at General Car Co. seeking an entry-level position in the supply chain at U.S. Pharmaceutical Co.

MY CAREER JOURNEY

Managing my career is my lifetime job. I have made more than twenty career pivots and several micro-changes in my life, so I know the struggle of searching for a new position, a new career, or a new company.

With each change, I built my knowledge and experience, which led me to create a method that got results, got job offers, and built meaningful careers. Each pivot I made was more focused and took less time. Colleagues advised me that finding a new role might take months, if not years. Using my Program, I made changes within weeks, not months. I am a believer; the Getting Hired Program works.

One of my early pivots took me from being a research biochemist to the manager of Information Technology. How did I do that? I started with a general goal of being a manager. I saw that the people who were making decisions and controlling the company's fate were in management positions. However, in the research department, that meant having a Ph.D., which I didn't have.

I set my goal, did my research, built my marketing campaign, and got moving. I asked managers that I knew, *"How did you get to be a manager?"* Years earlier, I decided that I would be the author of my future, and recognized that this was an opportunity to do just that.

Over the next few years, I worked through three pivots until I had secured my first management position. Two of the pivots were lateral to different departments, and one opportunity was a special project for a V.P. I knocked the special project out of the park. When the time was right, he offered me a management role in manufacturing.

The funny thing is that I turned it down because I received a second offer at the same time. The special project had also helped a Director of IT make some dramatic improvements. When the IT. Director heard that the V.P.. had offered me a job, he immediately offered me a job as a manager, which I accepted. The rest is history! The management career I wanted, took off.

Resources to Help You Prepare

The most important source of information about what you want in a career and what you are capable of doing in your work life is yourself. Be ready to spend some serious time in self-reflection about what you want in your future. In Chapter Two, the Magazine Article Exercise helps you outline your vision for your working life in some detail. Regardless of your career stage, this is a useful exercise.

For everything else, there are many resources to help. Online resources provide free information, guidance, and recommendations. Also, don't forget that many people can help, including your colleagues, family, and friends. It is all there, but you must take action. To be successful, you must be resilient and learn from your failures and be better prepared.

The results of being under-prepared are:

- Rejection emails – *"we will keep your resume on file."*
- You are ghosted after your interview – no email response at all.
- You are getting no interviews – with no opportunity to compete.
- You are being told that the position was filled (only to see the job listing still posted months later).
- You are being told that you are overqualified or under-qualified.
- You are finding no positions that fit your requirements or experience or your desired location.

If you experience some or all of these results during your search, this is an indicator that your preparation process is not working and needs to change. You can improve your results by reflecting and learning from each experience, and most importantly, taking an aggressive role to own and manage your career development.

GET READY TO SELL

In every career move, I used my current position to market myself. Getting the job you want, or even the job you need is all about selling yourself. Having a clear goal and knowing what is possible allows you to target your potential future employer, i.e., the person who needs someone who can solve their problem. They have work to do, and they need someone to do it, someone who can get the job done, i.e., someone like you.

The Getting Hired Program will help you get ready and succeed. The Program phases help you leverage your personal and professional background and show you how to utilize all of the resources at your fingertips to secure a role that will accelerate your career and ambitions. The Program is grounded in rigorous research methods, creative thinking, and personal marketing, with an intense focus on your goal. Being better prepared than your competition will give you the best chance of getting hired.

Chapter One Summary

- What is your next step? Decide what career stage you are in. The stages of a career are the lateral career stage, the promotion career stage, and the pivoting career stage.
- Be prepared to pivot your career either now or in the future, because career pivots are almost inevitable.
- Know what it means to pivot and how to make it happen.
- Make a list of potential pivots that you have considered.
- Make a list of the resources that can help you.

Chapter Two

MAKING THE MOST OF YOUR EXPERIENCE

Know thyself – Knowing yourself is the beginning of all wisdom. - Aristotle

You would be surprised how few people use all of their background and experience when trying to get hired. To be successful in your career, you need to be in the business of selling yourself, and to be better equipped to do that, you must accumulate everything you know about yourself and your experiences. Your career and your life is the amalgamation of all of your experiences. What you have done forms the foundation to create effective resumes, cover letters, marketing messages, and successful interviews.

If you think that you can't afford the time or effort to do the research, consider how much time you will waste and how much disappointment you will experience when you are unsuccessful in securing a meaningful job in your haste to be busy applying.

KNOW YOURSELF TO SELL YOURSELF

While pivoting from my job as a bench scientist in a university biochemistry laboratory to a corporate world position, I didn't know anything. I had never applied for a job, and thus, had to learn from scratch what I wanted, what was available, and how to apply. I also had to do some research on myself. I tried to write my resume and realized that I was horrible at selling myself. So, I decided to hire a career coach to help me get my marketing materials together. My coach interviewed me, asking detailed questions about my background, experiences, and accomplishments. She constructed a resume that made me stand out. A one-page resume was almost impossible at that time, and my new resume was four pages long.

GETTING HIRED

I searched for job listings and found five positions that I liked. I thoroughly examined each opportunity and organization, and with my new resume, I applied to all five posts. Within two weeks, I had five interviews, and over the next few weeks, I had five job offers. I was spoiled for choice, but I was pleased. My research paid off. I accepted my first job with a Fortune 100 company, and I intensely researched every career change I made after that.

To help you get to know yourself better, I've broken this chapter down into collecting your "cans" (information, skills, traits, education, experience), and your "wants." At the end of this section, you should have at least ten "wants," and "cans" consisting of five skills, three traits, and one industry. We are then able to begin to understand what your profile might look like.

Highlight Your Competencies, Skills and Traits

Make a list of everything that you are good at or have training in. Write one sentence for each item on the list describing how you have used this skill. Select the five skills in which you have the most experience. Include software experience, techniques, certifications, or any skill that you have had advanced training in (beyond typical university courses). If you consistently find a particular skill or certification required for the jobs you are applying for, consider getting certified. Then you can add "certification in process."

Traits are the foundation of who you are. Honesty, loyalty, detail-oriented, empathy, kindness, a strong work ethic, curiosity, skepticism, and friendliness are just a few traits that form a personality. Although traits are easy to claim, they are much more challenging to exemplify.

Make a list of your traits and select your three most important characteristics. Write three examples of how you have demonstrated that trait in your personal or professional life. These examples will be used to create your personal marketing message and your cover letters.

MAKING THE MOST OF YOUR EXPERIENCE

YOUR INDUSTRY EXPERIENCE AND INTEREST

Industry experience or knowledge forms an essential building block of where you want to take your career and where you can leverage your background. Experienced project managers in finance and manufacturing share many similarities. When a manufacturing company looks for a project manager, they will usually require manufacturing experience, and the same is true of financial institutions. Whether right or wrong, people who work within a given industry believe that no one can truly understand how to do a job if they haven't had the industry experience. I think that this tribal prejudice prevents many industries from acquiring new ideas or skills.

I spent almost 40 years providing consulting services to hospitals and healthcare systems. I should not have been surprised that hospital operational performance challenges have remained mostly unchanged during that same period. Healthcare recruiting routinely requires healthcare experience for healthcare managers, directors, and their executive teams; thus, a director who fails in one hospital may quickly find that same role in a different hospital, yet they may end up being unsuccessful there too. A sad story this may be, albeit not a surprising one either.

Enlightened leaders who look for the right person with the right skills to do the job with or without the specific industry experience are those whose organizations succeed. Some companies accomplish the injection of new knowledge and ideas by hiring consultants who have typically worked in multiple industries. I worked in 13 different sectors, which allowed me to bring various approaches to all of my clients.

So, you need to identify what industries interest you because, unless you are a consultant, you are likely to be in that industry for a long time. Where have you worked? What industry excites you? Make a list of all of the industry sectors where you have worked. If you have no work experience, what industries interest you the most?

GETTING HIRED

If you are pivoting your career, spend some significant time checking out the Bureau of Labor Statistics at www.bls.gov. This site has extensive information and data regarding jobs, careers, and industries. Which industry do you have the most depth of understanding and passion in? Your competencies, skills, traits, experience, and education make up what you "can" do. You will use these in making a career selection.

INTERVIEW THE FUTURE YOU

I have used this exercise with executives, managers, and recent graduates to identify what they want in their careers. The activity takes two to three hours to complete. Have fun with it, and think of what you want to be doing in the future.

Imagine that, ten years from now, you are interviewed for a published article about you and your career. Imagine that you are happier than you could ever imagine. Project yourself into the future and draft responses to the following questions:

1. What are your name and your current position?
2. How did you get to this place in your career?
3. Describe your typical day.
4. What are you most proud of?
5. What are the people like that you work with?
6. What are you most skilled at?
7. What do you wish you had known ten years ago?
8. Describe your work-life balance.
9. What is your vision for your career and your lifestyle?
10. What advice would you give to anyone beginning their career?

Once you have finished your draft, refine, and craft your story in the form of a news article, as if you are both the interviewer, and the interview subject. This exercise should be fun and informative.

MAKING THE MOST OF YOUR EXPERIENCE

When you are happy with the final product, print it out. Then, using a pen or marker, circle the words in your interview that are "wants," i.e., things that you need in your career to be happy. Make a list of these "wants."

With all of this preparation done, you now have the foundations to identify career options, choose a career path, and build your personal marketing materials to pursue the job that you want.

Chapter Two Summary

- Make a list of industries, those that you understand best, and those industries that you might consider.
- Review these industries using Bureau of Labor Statistics.
- List your competencies and skills that you have acquired throughout your life. Include soft skills (negotiation, collaboration, etc.) as well as hard skills (statistics, linear programming, jet engine repair, etc.)
- List your traits that will be of long term value to any company or team.
- Make a list of your "cans."
- Write a short description of how you have demonstrated each of your competencies, skills, and personal traits.
- Complete the "Interview of Your Future" Exercise. What new information did you discover, and how might you use it to frame your future career.
- Make a list of your "wants."

Chapter Three

COPING WITH STRESS

Action forces prioritization. If you're stuck deciding between options, force yourself to act. You can only act on one thing at a time, which means you will have to make something the top priority. Even if you pick wrong, you'll learn something. - James Clear

I have used a few techniques to control my reaction to the stress of unemployment and employment throughout my career. The six tactics that I have used most consistently and successfully are exercise, reading, writing, coaching, working, and planning.

Exercise Reduces Stress

Exercise is proven to reduce stress. A few years ago, I had just had my former employer, Arthur Andersen, collapsed under my feet. Another firm acquired my division, and my new role was in a technical area that was foreign to me. I had enormous pressure to succeed or be sacked.

My project was in Flagstaff, Arizona, and my team was intelligent, energetic, and also new to their roles. The workweeks were long with flights into Phoenix and then a two-hour drive at night to be on-site for an early morning start. The workdays were also long, but the team and I always found time for a meal and a workout. Before this, I told anyone who would listen, that I hated running and that I was not a "gym rat." By the time the project ended eight months later, I was both a runner and a gym rat. Getting out into the clean mountain air after work helped all of the stress melt away. I continued running throughout my career to cope with stress.

I won't bore you with all of the research to support the benefits of exercise in coping with stress, but invite you to do your experiment. For one week, go for a walk or run every morning to start your day and keep a diary of how you feel throughout the day. The next week go for a walk or run every evening after you finish your work and keep a log of how you feel. Choose which one works for you and keep track of your stress levels by simply writing down in the evening a number on a calendar between 1 and 10, with 1 indicating very low stress and ten being very high stress. Then adjust your routine to see how you can get the numbers to go down and stay down. What you measure will change.

READING CAN HELP YOU DECOMPRESS

Reading books on strategic thinking and novels can provide a simple way to get your stress levels to decrease. Once, I faced an exceptionally difficult person who was bent on destroying our project and our credibility by lying and deceit. I began reading the *Art of War* by Sun Tzu. One of the things that has stuck with me for years was the recommendation to never corner an opponent leaving no avenue for escape. The result is that your opponent will fight harder and stronger because they have nothing left to lose. That little piece of wisdom helped me successfully navigate a very tricky business problem. Find an inspiring book to read about business, history, or leadership and read a couple of pages a day.

WRITING IS THERAPEUTIC

My five-year contract in Australia was coming to an end, and I needed to find a new position somewhere in the world during the Great Recession of 2008. I had a new boss. My mentor was gone. My department's work had all but dried up, and the pressure to build revenue and find new clients was intense—lots of stress!

I developed a routine of starting my day early. I sat in a coffee shop and spent about 45 minutes each morning writing in a notebook by hand ideas, concepts, thoughts, and plans. This simple routine got me through the day, through the stress, and I still have that notebook with over a hundred pages of ideas.

I found it helpful to disconnect myself from technology by using pen and paper. Along the way I made lists. List are valuable for two reasons: first, a list helps you stop continually cycling through thoughts and second, a list gives you a simple road-map of things that you want to accomplish. Being paperless, I transcribed all of my lists into an Excel or Word format and always took a photo of the notes. Then I could throw them away and decluttered when I wanted.

Never underestimate the power of simple routines to create calm in your hectic life. Try spending at least twenty minutes every morning thinking about whatever you want to accomplish in your life. More importantly, write down the things that you want to achieve on this particular day. By taking control of your day from the start, you relieve significant pressure caused by the uncertainty and unknowns in life.

BOUNCE IDEAS OFF A COACH

I apologize in advance for this shameless self-promotion, but my clients have found comfort in having a career coach help them through their process of getting hired.

As a certified coach, I have worked with more than 500 individuals to help them progress their careers. I believe in the power of coaching. Coaching unlocks success and helps deliver meaningful results in challenging environments.

A coach can provide personalized guidance on meaningful job search strategies, resume and cover letter writing, career transitions, difficult conversations, team trust development, create ongoing, practical personal focus. Everyone has the resources within themselves to make meaningful changes and enhance their career. A coach's role is to catalyze the change that let people expand their strengths and focus their energy.

Find a career coach and request a complimentary chemistry session. The chemistry session is a shortened coaching session that will provide you with a preview of what to expect during a full coaching engagement.

GETTING HIRED

Most career and executive coaches will offer these meetings to see if there is good chemistry between client and coach.

Working While Looking

The longer you are out of work the more your stress levels soar. The obvious solution is to work. As silly as this *Catch-22* sounds there are some straight forward ways that you can work while looking. Three ways to work that will reduce stress are, part-time work, temporary staffing, and volunteering.

Part-time work is any job that pays you for less than full time hours. While this is not the ideal solution, part-time work has some definite benefits. Probably the greatest benefits of part-time work are that you have some income, and that it is easier to find a job when you have a job. Aside from those advantages, there are others.

Let's consider three of the many benefits. First, you build experience and add to your network. Second, the job appears on your resume and fills the gap in employment while demonstrating to perspective employers that you are ambitious and making the best use of your time. Third, because you are inside a company, working, you will have an inside track to fill any full time position that may become available.

Having some work is ultimately better than no work and paid part-time positions will relieve some of the financial stress. Because these positions are part-time and often contracted for a specific duration, you will still have time to do the work needed to get full time employment. The most enjoyable, productive, and profitable time in my career was when I was a contracted consultant. I was working three to four days a week on a wide variety of projects. I never went back to full-time work.

Temporary employment opportunities (temping) are typically offered by staffing agencies. You are probably thinking that these staffing agencies only focus on administrative roles, but you would be wrong. Temporary staffing agencies are often specialized and have needs for people at all levels and in all industries.

COPING WITH STRESS

At the more senior level, these roles are called interim. Interim assignments can be the CEO to fill a need for the sudden departure of a leader. They might also be an interim manager of an HR department to fill in for maternity leave. Specialized staffing agencies exist in almost every industry: Technology, manufacturing, healthcare, banking, hospitality, retail, and security to name just a few.

At the non-management level, staffing agencies fill positions for receptionists, general labor, construction, inventory control, drivers, cleaners, and the list goes on. These assignments can last a day, a week, or months. You have to be qualified and ready to work on a moments notice but sometimes the access that you get to new companies and people can be life changing. Don't overlook this strategy to both reduce stress and get hired.

You do not get paid for volunteering. So why would you want to volunteer? be important For the some of same reasons that temping and part-time work are helpful to your resume, network, and opportunities, volunteering can be helpful to your job seeking efforts. However, beyond these benefits, volunteering gives you something meaningful to do while you are looking. You will be around other people, you will build your experience and you will signal to your prospective employer that you can give as well as receive, all while reducing your level of stress. None of these tactics to reduce stress should be overlooked. But they all pale in comparison to the decrease in your stress levels that result from developing a plan to deal with crisis and fears.

PLAN FOR THE WORST AND HOPE FOR THE BEST

Looking for a new job or transitioning to a new career can be frightening. We all have fears; some are real, others imagined. The fear of falling off a cliff is real and has real consequences. The fear that the earth will suddenly split open and you fall into a never-ending abyss is imagined (although it could happen if you live in California). Fear can paralyze you and cause you to stress, and stress amplifies your fear. This

Crisis Management exercise will help you identify some of your fears and create a plan to address the fear. These plans can serve you forever.

CRISIS MANAGEMENT BY HARNESSING YOUR FEARS

What's the very worse thing that can happen? What result do you fear most? What are you worried about? – Write all of them down. Focus on what might happen within the next month or so and on things that are not the consequence of something else happening. For example: *"I am afraid that I will lose my job"* or *"I'm afraid I'm in the wrong career."*

Don't expand beyond that initial event – we will do that in the next step. Use short bullet points/headlines. Pay attention to what is deep inside your head. What are the things that you are afraid might happen very soon? What fears are you hesitant to admit to yourself. Did you capture everything?

Action: Create a list and put the number one next to the biggest, scariest one. Then label numbers two and three in order of priority.

ANTICIPATION AND EXPECTATIONS

Action: Write your number one fear on the center left-hand side of a piece of paper. If your number one worst thing does happen, what are the expected consequences that you fear? Write the direct consequences to the right of the fear. Each consequence is now a fear. What is the result of each of these consequences? This becomes a series of *"if this happens, then that might happen, and if that happens, then this other bad thing happens."* Don't overlook being proactive. If I think I might lose my job, what can I do to prevent that or prepare for that? But follow the expected consequences, always selecting the worst-case scenario. Prepare for the worse, and the rest will be much easier.

For example: *"If I lose my job, I might never get a job, and if I don't ever get a job then I will run out of money, if I run out of money then I might have to sell my house."* Don't go beyond four layers of expected consequences for each of your fears. The result will look like a tree on its side with the branches flowing to your page's right.

Make a list of what you expect to happen if your fears become real. Start with your top three fears, only. For each of the consequences – outline a simple, proactive plan of action

"And if that happens, WHAT WILL I DO"?

Don't overlook being proactive. If I think I might lose my job, what can I do to prevent that or prepare for that? But follow the expected consequences, always selecting the worst-case scenario. Prepare for the worse, and the rest will be much easier.

This is process creates all of your Plan B's for all of your major, realistic fears. Plan A is what you want to happen; what you will do if your fear never occurs. Plan B is what you will do if the fear event does occur, and Plan A doesn't work out.

A common trap is doing everything sequentially. So we have our Plan A, and only when that doesn't pan out, do we think about Plan B. In essence, we only ever work on Plan A's. Sequential or linear actions can waste time and cause a roller-coaster of both results and emotions. To avoid this roller-coaster start working on your Plan B, while you are implementing Plan A.

So in the example, Plan A is that you don't lose your job. Hooray! You can pursue your career/role with the confidence that you have a Plan B. If you know that the worse (fear) MIGHT happen, what actions can you take now to prepare yourself for that. What steps can you take to prevent the worse from happening; what might you do?

Think exhaustively and create a detailed list of next steps. Decide what to do first. Make a specific, comprehensive plan of steps to take NOW — day 1; week 1; month 1.

For example: *"If I know that I will lose my job, I will identify other options, contact my network, let my friends and family know, etc."* or *"If I know that I won't ever get a job (in a specific time-frame I will:*

GETTING HIRED

- Investigate other careers
- Go back to school
- Start a business
- Other

"If I know that I would run out of money, I will:
- Sell the house
- Get a loan
- Get any job
- Other"

CREATE A DETAILED ACTION PLAN

It is not enough to have a plan; you must take action, and as you take action revisit your plan and make it better. But the number one key to success is action. Consistent, effective action on an imperfect plan is far superior to no action on a perfect plan.

REVIEW AND REFINE YOUR PLAN

Complete your action plan and review your progress frequently. In the first few days, this review should occur daily. This is your plan, and you should update it and change it as you see things need to change. Your biggest fear now is that you don't follow through with the actions that you have laid out. What do you do if that happens? Circle back to the top continually and make sure that you are focused on the right things. The more you refine your plan, the better the plan will be, and the better the results will be. Keep your plan current and relevant. Make changes, additions, modifications to your plan frequently.

True story, I had just been given a raise and expanded responsibilities, so on the next Sunday my wife and I sat down on a park bench (below is the actual bench) and went through this exercise because we were tired of our *"but, what if?"* conversations. When we had finished, we felt much better because we had the skeleton of a Plan B for our most significant *"what ifs?"*

On Wednesday of the next week, I woke up and went to the office to continue with my Plan A. The previous Friday I had been given a raise, a small bonus, and responsibility for building a new product line. Plan A was to create a new product line strategy and review it with my local department head.

I had a morning meeting to review my plan with my boss. When I arrived, an HR. representative was sitting in on the meeting. Without any warning, my department and my role of nine years was eliminated. Plan A was, in that very moment, obliterated. I was shocked. By early afternoon I had already begun working on Plan B.

I was lucky. The next time something out of the blue happened, I wasn't lucky...I was prepared! If you think your worse fear might happen, develop your Plan A to prevent your worse fear from happening in the first place. This will be your proactive prevention plan, and this plan is superior to any Plan B., But if and when your Plan A fails, you have to have a Plan B.

Chapter Three Summary

- Create a stress management plan that includes doing some or all five strategies to reduce daily stress: exercise, reading, writing, and planning.
- Create a daily routine of good habits.
- Make daily, weekly, and monthly to-do lists and check off everything.
- Complete your crisis management exercise.
- The most effective way to reduce stress is to be better prepared.
- Develop your Plan B for every fear that you have.
- Don't neglect your Plan A. This is your plan of action to prevent your fears from becoming a reality. If your fears are never realized, you still need a plan.

Chapter Four

IDENTIFYING YOUR CAREER OPTIONS

Never do things others can do and will do if there are things others cannot do or will not do. - Amelia Earhart

Before you begin any job search, take the time to consider what kind of working life you want. You may not be excruciatingly specific, but at least you can establish a general direction. What is your long-term objective?

In Chapter Two, you identified the two factors to consider when selecting a career path: What you want to do, and what you can do. If there is no gap between these two factors, you can then take a straight line to your goal. In most cases, there is a gap; for example, if you want to be a manager, but have no management experience. When there is a gap between want and can, you will need to find a way to improve your capabilities to succeed.

What are your career options? What may sound like a boring career can turn out to be very exciting, and vice versa. This is why some research is critical. You need to know what a particular career entails. What are the jobs and paths to advancement?

Your career is the sum of a series of roles, responsibilities, and experiences. You may be looking for the same type of job that you just left or pivoting to a different career. Each stage in your career will pose different challenges.

WHAT CAREER STAGE ARE YOU IN?

If you are not looking for your next position, you will become stagnant. By not managing your career path, you run the risk of being at the mercy of others. At the very least, you should have a Plan B if something out of your control happens to your current firm or your current position. Since companies can fail, be bought out, or be restructured or downsized, as the owner of your career, you must be prepared and have a Plan B, regardless of your career stage.

What is your next step? What stage are you in? Are you preparing for a Lateral move, a Promotion, or a Pivot? If you are unclear about your career stage, refer to Chapter One for a description of each phase.

At any stage, your options can seem overwhelming. Most options come with strings attached, such as salary reduction, steep learning curves, title reduction, and other changes that make the decision more challenging. Any career pivot is a challenging adventure that usually comes with some risks. Often, people do not think in terms of their long-term career objectives, and instead, succumb to being short-sighted and opportunistic. Short-term thinking may result in accepting a position for money, a title, or prestige that ends up being a dead end. No progress is made towards a career goal, or worse, failure in a job that has gone off course. Again, this is about the gap between want and can.

To keep moving in your chosen direction requires planning. Carefully thinking about what you want and laying out a strategy to get you, there will create stability in your career.

On my journey, where I went from Project Manager to Vice President of Operations, I once took a position as an entry-level consultant, which paid half as much for twice the work. The path to your destination will never be a straight line; therefore, you have to be agile, flexible. You do what you have to do to reach your objective, which is why you need to have some idea of what the goal is before you start searching for a job.

Research the Careers That Interest You

Search for the careers that interest you, i.e., careers with jobs that you want to do. Look up the Wikipedia description of the professions you are interested in. Also, check out the Bureau of Labor Statistics (BLS) for career outlooks at https://www.bls.gov/ooh/. BLS is a great

IDENTIFYING YOUR CAREER OPTIONS

place to look if you are not sure what career might interest you. Many experienced managers, directors, and executives find themselves burned out or bored with their current job. What do they want to do? What can they do? The options are endless, and sorting through them can take some time. The Bureau of Labor Statistics has data on careers and industries that provide many ideas for you to consider. Their website has descriptions of the outlook for different jobs with projections of growth and salaries. Keep a list of anything that interests you.

Use Google to search for some of the job titles that interest you. Look through the search results and adjust your search using different versions of the same job title (e.g., project management, project manager, program manager, project specialist, project leader). Companies have different job titles for the same role or function. To help you narrow your career objectives, you can use these same methods to research job openings, careers, and industries. Keep a list of any job title that interests you.

Research the companies that use people with your skills. Go into enough depth to understand the company and have a good sense of its reputation and culture. Reach out to people on LinkedIn who work at these companies and ask this simple question: *"I would like to connect with you to learn more about X company."* This approach will not be 100% successful, but you will get some contacts. From there, you can ask further questions about the company and the particular career at that company. Keep a list of every company that interests you.

CONSULTING FIRMS HIRE A WIDE VARIETY OF PROFESSIONS

Consulting is a good career choice for both new and experienced professionals. Experienced professionals may want to change where and how they work. New graduates may like to explore career options before committing to a path. Consulting provides a variety of work environments, industries, professions, and opportunities. Consulting is the subject of my next book in my Career series – *Being a Consultant*.

GETTING HIRED

"The number of people employed in management consulting in the United States has grown annually over the past five years, and in 2018 there were around 684,470 management consultants employed in the U.S. Despite the increasing number of consultants, finding and keeping good employees was one of the top business challenges for management consulting firms. The most pressing issue for companies was, by far, attracting and developing new businesses, with 79 percent of senior managers citing this a leading challenge." (Statistica.com)

ACCOUNTING FIRMS ARE LARGE EMPLOYERS

The top four accounting firms employ more than one million people and hire thousands of professionals each year. Some of the people they hire are accountants, but not all. Have a look at their websites and look at the career, jobs, or *"work with us"* sections and you will find a wide variety of career options. Most of these firms also have advisory practices (consulting). Advisory practices also hire a wide variety of professionals with different skills and backgrounds.

USE LINKEDIN PREMIUM RESOURCES

If you haven't already done so, sign up for LinkedIn Premium, which gives you access to on-demand learning, exclusive email, who is looking at you, expanded job search features, and better visibility in the marketplace. Later, when you have focused on a few select job titles, you can set the Job Notification option on LinkedIn to send you daily updates on newly-posted positions.

Using multiple job platforms to do your searches will help you to see trends and patterns. Make a note of these, look for the same job across all the platforms, and set notifications for them. Later, when you narrow down what tools work best for you and your chosen career, you can eliminate or refine these notifications. Look for companies looking for many roles. Look for the same roles but in different locations.

Pause Before You Start Applying

You can waste much time chasing those first job openings and get nowhere. If you are a glutton for punishment, knock yourself out. However, if you follow the Getting Hired Program, you will get offers, and if you get offers, you will have choices, and choices mean that you will get not just take any job, but rather the job you want, and you will avoid a lot of pain and suffering in the process.

Doing this exercise by yourself can be very challenging to embark upon. The trick is to think freely and create an exhaustive list of options. To narrow your list down and make a selection requires some deep thinking and soul searching to identify what matters to you.

If there is a gap between a career that you want to do and what you can do, your career plan must consider how you intend to close that gap by acquiring new capabilities and skills.

Chapter Four Summary

- Write down what career stage you are in. If you know the career stage you are in, you will know whether you need to identify career options.
- Be curious and see what else is out there.
- Make an exhaustive list of career options by continuing your research on the Bureau of Labor Statistics and Wikipedia.
- Search the Internet for information about different careers that appeal to you and the profession you are currently in.
- Sign up for LinkedIn Premium.
- Keep detailed notes on everything you find.
- Don't apply for anything just yet. There are more information and knowledge that you need to collect.

Chapter Five

LEARN ABOUT THE JOB MARKET

Research your ideas. See if there is a demand. Many people have great ideas, but they don't know if there is a need for it. You also have to research your competition. – **Magic Johnson**

The job market is driven by companies that are hiring. For the career options that you are considering, you need to know who is hiring and where the jobs are. First, you need to find out the job titles that belong to those options. Even if you are already working in your chosen career but want a new job, you need to do some job market research. Next, you need to determine who the major companies are that are hiring.

You will either find your new job on the Internet or through a contact. Getting Hired helps you learn about your preferred job market to develop a successful job search campaign. Your job market research will identify specific job titles, companies that are hiring, people who are hiring, and locations that have opportunities. You also need to look through your contacts to find someone who can help. Your objective is to find a career and a job that you want and are qualified for, and then get in front of someone who can hire you.

Networking: About 60% of all jobs are filled by individuals who either recommended, know someone, or are referred to the hiring manager. So, you need to focus some of your energy in finding out who the people are, and with whom you need to connect.

Applying online: About 40% of jobs are filled through an online application, so you will also need to do this. Your results will improve when you find the positions that best meet your background, experience, and career objectives. You want to find a job that you want

GETTING HIRED

and for which you are qualified. If your search is ineffective, you won't find openings that are the best match, and ultimately, you will miss out.

Use Google to conduct your first search. Start a search with the career title and the word *"jobs"* tagged on to the end (e.g., project management becomes *"project management jobs"*). Begin your search with as few filters as possible (e.g., location select *"anywhere"* and everything else set to "all"). If you narrow your geographical area to your particular location, you may inadvertently miss jobs with headquarters in other places or positions that are highly paid but in different cities. When conducting any type of research, the rule of thumb is to start broad and narrow your focus. You can do this research very quickly, and you need to keep copious notes so that you don't have to do repetitive work.

For the research you are doing for each career, look at who is hiring and for which jobs within that career. The following list comprises a handful of the online platforms for job openings that you can use for your career research:

- Careers.Google.com
- Monster.com
- Indeed.com
- Jobseeker.com
- Careerbuilder.com
- LinkedIn.com
- Glassdoor.com
- Ziprecruiter.com
- RobertHalf.com
- Neuvoo.com
- Zippia.com
- Handshake.com

LEARN ABOUT THE JOB MARKET

When you find something (e.g., a job title, a company, a location, a recruiter) when doing your market research, make a note to use this information when creating your future job search campaign.

After you have selected some job titles, companies, and careers that interest you, your preliminary search should be as general as possible to determine what is available and of interest. Note that this is not your job search, this is your market research. You want to find out who is hiring, what kinds of jobs, how many are available, and where these companies are located.

ONCE AGAIN, PAUSE BEFORE YOU START APPLYING

Don't apply yet! There is more work to do! Before you are ready to apply online, you need to continue to Phase 2 of the Getting Hired Program. In this Phase you will create a method to make a choice and finally choose what career options where you want to put 100% of your focus.

Chapter Five Summary

- Make a list of the most common job titles using Google for your first searches.
- Make a detailed list of the companies hiring in each of the career options you are considering.
- Find people on LinkedIn who might help you understand different careers and ask for advice.
- Search for your job titles of choice on job search platforms. Keep track of overlap of job postings and common recruiting platforms for those jobs. Sign up for 5 to 7 job search platforms.
- Search on LinkedIn for the companies that interest you and spend some time on each of their websites.
- Search on LinkedIn for people who work at the companies that you have identified and who have jobs similar to what you would like to do – connect with them and ask for information about the career; don't ask for a job.
- Set aside a designated amount of time each day to do job market research.
- Your goal is to be a knowledge expert in your job market.
- Don't apply for anything just yet. There are more information and knowledge that you need to collect.

THE GETTING HIRED PROGRAM

PHASE 2 - FOCUS

MAKING A SMART DECISION

Chapter Six

HOW TO CHOOSE A CAREER

Do not go where the path may lead, go instead where there is no path and leave a trail. – **Ralf Waldo Emerson**

Most of my clients are at a crossroads in their careers. They ask themselves, "What can I do? What should I do? What else is possible?" There are so many ideas and options that they think their biggest challenge is choosing something. But it is not! Their biggest challenge is staying focused. When the focus is lost, progress is slow or non-existent.

It can be fun and exciting to envision being a rock star or a Pulitzer prize-winning author, or a travel blogger, and these are all possible. But are they probable? The work and talent to become any of these or any profession other than your current career are exponentially greater. Change is hard. Incredible change is incredibly hard.

Don't Let an Abundance of Options Stop You

Often, we do this type of brainstorming to distract us from the reality that we need to focus and do the hard work to find our next step in our career. Couple this with the uncertainty of, "Will I get a job in my current career? Will I like my new job? Can I compete? Is this the right job?"

Once, when I was in transition, I thought it would be great to be a day-trader. So, I read and studied and did some experimentation and some "paper trading" and decided to go all in. We had high-speed wiring routed into our home. I signed up for a state of the art trading platform. I opened an account to trade S&P Futures and was on my way. Living on the West Coast, I had to get up early in the morning to prepare for the opening bell of the New York Stock Exchange.

Everything went well until it didn't. I failed to realize that professionals are doing this full time on the trading floor that I was competing with. They wanted to make money as much or more than I did. The difference was that they were playing with other people's money. I was playing with my family's money. It all came crashing down one afternoon when a trade I placed bottomed out, and I lost the money I couldn't afford to lose. I underestimated how difficult it would be to learn something so completely different from my career as a management consultant. I refocused and spent the next 20 years consulting and earning back what I had lost in time and money.

So, with all of the ideas swimming around in your head, you lose focus on the goal: getting hired. So how do you regain focus? You regain focus by getting organized and having a process to follow.

You choose by first identifying all of the options and ideas and writing them all down. This slows down the endless mental review of options that adds to your anxiety. Next, create a systematic criteria for making your decision and then using these criteria to generate a shortlist. Then lastly, focus in on your top two until you can confidently choose your direction.

How do You Make Choices

Choosing something and making a decision about the various options available is a very personal thing. Do you make choices with your head or with your heart? I recommend that you blend the two, the head and heart. To do this, you will create the criteria that you will use to make your decision.

Your heart will tell you what you want, what you feel good about, what you would be proud to do, and what you are passionate about. Your head will tell you what you can do, as well as what specific educational and work experience, capabilities, skills, and unique personality traits you want to use. If there is a gap between a career you want and what you can do, your choice must consider how you might close that gap.

In this phase, you will establish your criteria for selecting realistic candidates for careers. You will then apply those criteria, weed out the options that don't fit and make a choice.

Most of my clients struggle with this phase and have gotten value from working with a career coach to help them work through this process. If you look deep inside yourself to find what really matters to you and then remain flexible and vigilant, you will then discover where you can take your career and have added confidence.

CREATE YOUR SELECTION CRITERIA

To create a selection criteria, you can go back and review the research that you did in previous chapters. Once you have done this, write down your list of criteria based on the answers to these questions:

Six questions to help you define what you "want" in your career:

1. Can you think of something that you achieved and are proud of? Something that you did well?

2. When have you felt proud, confident, and energized?

3. What do you love about your current situation?

4. What would you change, if anything, in your current situation to make you love it more?

5. What is the goal for your next career move, either internally or externally?

6. What do you want your career, job, and life to look and feel like next year?

Use the answers to these questions to create a criteria list. Score each one of them using the following scale. Where one is not important, and ten is critical to my happiness and success, ask yourself, how important is this issue to me?

I would recommend that you construct this list in an Excel spreadsheet. Once you have scored all of these criteria, organize them by placing them in order from the highest to the lowest. Select any five criteria that score eight or greater. These are your "WANT" criteria.

During the "Get to Know Yourself" chapter, you identified five skills. These are your "CAN" criteria.

NOW YOU ARE READY TO CREATE A SHORTLIST

There are many ways to make a decision. Everyone has their method that has worked for them in the past. Some prefer a gut decision, whereas others prefer an analytical decision. I can pretend to guide you in making a gut decision, but I do have one piece of advice: after you have made your decision, sleep on it and see if you feel the same in the morning. If you feel the same, go for it! If, however, you feel differently, then try this more analytical approach.

From your list of options, you are now ready to score each one against your selection criteria. This should be a straightforward exercise. Make a list of your options down the left side of an Excel spreadsheet or a piece of paper. Next, write your six "Want" criteria and your five "Can" criteria across the top as column headers. Now, score each of the career options against each of the criteria. Place a "1" or "0" in each cell. A "1" means that this career meets the criterion exactly. A "0" means that this career is a less than perfect fit.

Calculate the total of all the scores for each career and select the top three careers/job titles. If you find more than three career options, repeat the exercise with the highest-scoring careers. This time, score each of the criteria from 0 to 3, where zero means that the occupation doesn't match the criteria at all, a "1" means there is some fit, but it is low, "2" means that there is a strong fit, and "3" is a perfect fit.

Make a total of the scores for each career and select the top three careers/job titles. If you still have more than three, choose the three with the highest score for the "want" criteria. Which three roles or job titles are the MOST appealing? Which of these roles make you feel energized? This is because you can train skills, but you can't teach passion.

You now have a shortlist of three jobs, roles, or job descriptions that you find the most appealing. The next step is to do some more research, get more focused, and choose one from this list to focus all of your efforts on. Your career path will be smoother if you are focused because whatever you focus on, you will get.

Chapter Six Summary

- Commit yourself to complete the work in this chapter within a week and hold yourself accountable.
- Make a complete list of your career options based on the research you completed in Phase One.
- Make a list of all of your dreams and ideas related to your career.
- Create your career "Wants."
- Create your career "Cans."
- Review your "Wants" and "Cans" and determine your scoring values.
- Create an Excel spreadsheet and score your career options.
- Using the scores, select the highest scoring options to choose the top three Short List of career/job title options.
- Investigate LinkedIn for connections that you may already have with people in companies that focus on the careers that are on your shortlist.

Chapter Seven

SELECTING YOUR CAREER

The trouble lies in the fact that people do not have an objective, one thing they stick to, letting all else go. Success is the product of the severest kind of mental and physical application. - Thomas Edison

For your top three job titles/roles, do some significant research on each and keep detailed records. What do you need to know? What do you need to learn? What will make you confident that these are the right three job titles? Making any choice is very personal. Having choices is the ultimate freedom. So why is choosing so difficult? One thing that can inhibit a definitive choice is the fear that the choice you make is wrong. While you can never predict the future, you can definitely choose how you respond to the future.

Suppose that you decide that you will change your company rather than pursue a promotion within the company where you currently work. There are an infinite number of unknown possibilities that you may face in the future. The new company could go bankrupt and you loose your job. The company you left could struggle financially and you avoid being laid off. The new company wins an unexpected contract and you are promoted. The old company goes public and you would have been an instant millionaire. You never know what will happen.

What you can know is that you would have a plan and be prepared for unexpected as well as predicted change. The best advice I can give you is to do your homework, make a choice, and then give that choice 100% of your effort to make it work for you. Meanwhile have your second and third options on a back burner and be agile. You might make what you feel is the best choice but be faced by insurmountable circumstances that require a change in direction.

A QUICK EXERCISE

For a quick exercise, try saying out loud: *"Hi, I'm (Your Name), and I am a (job title)."*

How does it make you feel? Why does it make you feel that way?

I know that some of you are saying, *"Hey, Paul. I don't have time for all this navel-gazing, I just need a job."* Sure, you do! But if you don't get this phase right, you may not get a job. And if you do get a job, sooner or later, you will be going through this process again. The old saying goes, *"Measure twice and cut once."* Studies have shown that when the amount of planning and preparation is increased, the shorter the project's overall duration. If you do your research, it will take you less time to get the job of your dreams. After all, how can you get the position of your dreams if you don't take the time to dream?

When researching your top three job titles/roles, learn the following topics in detail:

- Description of the career progression
- Number of openings nationwide
- Number of opportunities in your location
- Salary ranges
- Career outlook; future growth for each career
- Top ten companies who employ people with those careers
- Qualifications required for the profession, from entry-level to the most senior level

Write a paragraph describing how your background, experience, and skills meet your chosen career requirements.

ASK FOR HELP WHEN YOU NEED HELP

Embarking on this exercise without help can be challenging. The trick is to think freely and create an exhaustive list of options. Narrowing down your list and making a selection requires some deep thinking and soul searching to identify what matters to you.

Once you have established your realistic candidates for careers, you can then apply those criteria and weed out the two options that don't fit. Most of my clients struggle with this part and have gotten value from working with a career coach to help them work through this process. If you look deep inside yourself to find what matters to you and then remain flexible and vigilant, you will discover where you can take your career with confidence.

In general, taking a job that you are passionate about but not fully qualified for is not as big a problem as selecting a career that you are highly qualified for, but hate.

Chapter Seven Summary

- Do the "Hi I am Fred, and I am a (fill in the job title) at (fill in a prestigious company)" exercise – write down how you feel for each version on you shortlist.
- Do some preliminary research on each of the three careers/job titles from your Short List including:
    - Career progression,
    - Number of job openings,
    - Number of openings in your location,
    - Salary ranges,
    - Career outlook,
    - Top ten companies, and
    - Qualifications required.
- For each of the three, write a paragraph describing how your background and experience ("cans") fit the needs of the career path or job titles.
- For each of the three, describe how each of the career paths meets your "wants."

Chapter Eight

BECOME AN EXPERT IN YOUR SELECTED CAREER

We must see our true selves with an open mind, and when we think of things – when there are things we want to do – we must do them as if our lives depend on it. – Shunmyo Masuno

Now that you have done all of your research and investigation and identified your options, narrowed them down further, and decided, it is time to do some more in-depth study. This research is very specific, and the amount of effort you put into knowing about your career choice will reflect your passion. Potential employers will quickly recognize your interest in learning as much as possible about your chosen job/career. Remember that your potential employer is an expert in this career. Your goal should be to demonstrate that you are a passionate student of their industry/career and career path.

INTENSE CAREER RESEARCH

The Career Specific Background Research Exercise is a starting point to become an expert in your career choice. To describe this exercise, I use the term *"industry"* as a generic term for any industry. When completing this exercise, you will substitute your personal industry choice for general services. For example, if you choose the financial services industry, the instruction below would read, "Understand financial services companies in more detail."

1. Understand industry companies in more detail:
   - What are they, and what exactly do industry companies do?
   - What industries are they working in or with?
   - Draw a flow chart of their relationship to their industry (if

you are unfamiliar with flow charts, seek out some simple YouTube videos or instructions through a Google search).

- What is the business advantage of a industry company? Why do they exist?
- How do industry companies differ from other companies in their industry?
- What is the future of industry and trends?
- Who are the primary customers/clients of industry?

2. Search recent consulting reports on industry companies and write a one page summary of each report.
    - Delloite
    - PWC
    - KPMG
    - EY
    - Others

3. List the top 10 industry companies by revenue in the US.
4. Research each of the ten companies exhaustively and include:
    - Headquarters location
    - CEO or President
    - US and global locations
    - Mission and Vision
    - Number of employees
    - Dollars in net profit/expenses/revenue
    - All services they provide
    - Corporate structure
    - Leadership team
    - Recent news
    - Other essential data or information

5. What are the three primary risks faced by these industry companies?

6. Describe which of your skills would be important to industry companies.

7. After all of your research, describe your own opinions about the industry.

Your objective with this research exercise is to demonstrate to yourself and anyone that might interview you that you understand the business, have taken the time to prepare, are committed, care, and are willing to do hard work to succeed. These traits are highly valued by all industries and hiring managers.

As you proceed to learn, keep extensive notes, and draft/write up your company profile as a complete summary of your research and opinions. This research on your chosen career path and industry will help you create your marketing package for subsequent applications and interviews

Chapter Eight Summary

- Make a conscious decision that you will become the most knowledgeable person in your chosen career.
- Find out who knows more than you about this career and ask for help and advice.
- Make a list of people on LinkedIn who have jobs that you want and review their profiles and resumes.
- Make a list of the expected competencies, training, skills, and other requirements for the level above the job title that you are focusing on.
- Keep extensive, organized notes on everything you find.

THE GETTING HIRED PROGRAM

PHASE 3 - PREPARE

CREATING A MARKETING PACKAGEAKING

Chapter Nine

CREATE A PERSONAL MARKETING MESSAGE

I've learned that people will forget what you said, people will forget what you did, but people will never forget how you made them feel. - Maya Angelou

Just as your resume is your physical calling card, your Personal Marketing Message (PMM) is your verbal calling card. Get your Personal Marketing Message right, and you will make a great first impression. Frequently called an "elevator pitch," your Personal Marketing Message should help you quickly make an impact. You can also use many elements of your PMM as an introduction in your resume, cover letter, phone calls, or meetings or networking events when asked to introduce yourself. In an abbreviated version, you can use your PMM to answer the "What do you do?" question when meeting new friends. Of course, this is just a jumping-off point.

You can expand, add detail, and tailor your message to your audience. Whom are you talking to? How much do they care? Adjust what you say to suit the person.

DEVELOP YOUR CONTENT

Developing an agile Personal Marketing Message starts by creating a menu of content for each of the following:

- Introduction - your name.
- What is your headline?
- What are you most famous for?
- A couple of your stories of success.

GETTING HIRED

- What do you know about the person/company/other (but don't tell them whom they are, they know who they are)? Tell them why they are exciting or what makes them different to you.
- What role or career are you looking for?
- What are you passionate about?
- How do you add value?
- What can you do for the company?
- What have you done?
- What unique experience have you had?
- Your professional experience.
- Your degree.

DRAFT YOUR PERSONAL MARKETING MESSAGE

Draft separate, individual sentences for each of the following items, making sure that the sentences are concise and powerful.

- Choose an item from your menu.
- Include your OFFER: add value to the team, help enhance processes, manage projects on time and on budget, reduce cost, build teamwork (this is the answer to the "Why should I hire you?" question that is in their head).
- Don't forget to include your "ASK." This is where you ask for something (depending, obviously, on the situation). Examples of what you can ask for:
- A meeting: either in-person or in a call to discuss more.
- A contact: for networking.
- Information: related to the industry or role.
- Advice: recommendations on what to do next.
- An email address: for follow up and continued contact.
- A visit to the company: to further understand their business.

CREATE A PERSONAL MARKETING MESSAGE

Your entire pitch should take no more than 30 seconds to deliver at a conversational speed. To review and check the timing, go to MS Word use Review > Read Aloud – How does it sound to you?

Practice - Practice

The practice is what will make your Personal Marketing Message part of you. The better you know it, the more comfortable you will be when introducing yourself to the world.

- Revise and repeat.
- Now try it yourself. Your tone should be enthusiastic, upbeat, confident, friendly.
- Practice in front of a mirror.
- Practice with friends and family and ask for feedback.
- Smile!
- Refine and memorize the content, not using the exact words or order.
- Make a recording of your PMM. This is Recording A.
- Practice, practice, practice.
- Experiment with the order until you can start anywhere and go anywhere.
- Experiment with different content and different orders.

As mundane and tedious as all of this sounds, the time and effort you put into your PMM will pay dividends when you are under pressure, and first impressions are critical.

Two Essentials for a Powerful PMM

Two essential skills that will help you to deliver a powerful Personal Marketing Message are:

1. **Know Your PMM – COLD!** - Knowing your PMM so well that you can improvise the order and content to meet the needs of the situation (it doesn't need to be the same every time), and

2. **Deliver your PMM with Energy and Passion** - When you deliver your PMM, you must get yourself into the right frame of mind and be able to get in that same frame of mind quickly, on the spot. People get energy when they are talking with people who exhibit passion, and they pay attention.

ENHANCE THE PASSION OF YOUR DELIVERY

To get into the right frame of mind and experience the level of energy you need when delivering your Personal Marketing Message, think of a subject, hobby, interest, or any topic that makes you happy, excited, or know a lot about (not work). Let's call it "your passion." Something that you are passionate about. Your passion could be a sport, a hobby, a movie, a book, a TV show, a road trip, a family gathering, or anything that you are confident in your knowledge and feelings and gets you excited.

1. Take a few minutes to create your story.
2. Tell us about passion 1: Spend 30 seconds to tell someone about "Your thing." Begin with "I'm excited about X because…"
3. Tell us about passion 2: Imagine that the person you are telling knows nothing about your subject, repeat "Your passion."
4. Tell us passion 3: Next, go over-the-top and repeat "Your passion" as if you are telling the audience at Super Bowl during the half time show.

Without a pause, recite your Personal Marketing Message. Keep the same energy as in number 4 above. This is the energy that you should have when you are introducing yourself. Think about this: if you are not excited about yourself, how can you expect someone else to be passionate about you? Remember, no one knows you as you know you.

CREATE A PERSONAL MARKETING MESSAGE

HAVE FUN WITH IT.

Immediately make a second recording of you delivering your PMM. This is Recording B. When you listen to Recording B, ask yourself if this person sounds like someone I want to know more about. Does this person exude confidence in themselves? (Displaying confidence is what you are going for. It may not surprise you to know that when you display confidence, you feel confident. Act the way you want to feel).

Compare Recording B with Recording A. If Recording B is not more convincing, repeat the "Your passion" exercise until your new recording is much more energetic than your original Recording A.

PRACTICE AND ENJOY

If you are not excited and enthusiastic about yourself, don't expect others to be, so get excited every time you do your Personal Marketing Message.

Chapter Nine Summary

- Draft your personal marketing message.
- Develop the Two Essentials for a Powerful PMM.
- People remember candidates that are excited about themselves and their career.
- Complete the "your thing" exercise that creates passion in your delivery.
- Practice your PMM with at least three people .
- Practice your PMM in random order.
- Use MS Word - Review - Read Aloud.
- Time your message - target 30 sec.
- Practice and record yourself.
- Make a video of yourself delivering your message; refine your message and your body language.
- Practice your PMM every chance you have, with everyone you can, until it is second nature.

Chapter Ten

GETTING YOUR RESUME TO THE RIGHT PERSON

A little simplification would be the first step toward rational living, I think. – Eleanor Roosevelt

Now that you have completed your research, you are better prepared to create your marketing package and sell yourself. Your marketing package consists of all of the client-facing elements that you need to sell yourself. Your package will include three critical tools: your personal marketing message, resume, and cover letter. Once created, you will update these tools throughout your career, even when you are not looking to change jobs.

Your resume is only a part of your total personal marketing package. Your personal marketing materials' three primary components are your resume, your cover letter, and your Personal Marketing Message. Your personal marketing message is critical to having success when you apply for open positions, so you need to get all three of these correct.

Major organizations and small companies alike invest in hiring the best candidates for their needs. The process begins with the manager in charge of the hiring decision writing a job posting. The job description is often a combination of the resume of the person currently filling the role or leaving the position and the formal job description that resides in Human Resources (HR). The hiring manager will sometimes tweak the job posting by adding skills, duties, or requirements that have been lacking or desirable. Once the job is posted, a recruiter or HR representative must then find qualified candidates. This is where you get to introduce yourself by way of your resume.

GETTING HIRED

A recruiter, HR representative, or hiring manager may spend very little time looking at your resume before deciding to interview you. So your resume has to be clear, complete, and concise. However, before your resume reaches their desk, an automated artificial intelligence (AI) Applicant Tracking System (ATS) will most likely have screened your resume and the hundreds, if not thousands, of other resumes.

WHERE DOES YOUR RESUME GO

To understand how to assure that you have a fair chance of being selected for a job, your resume needs to get to the right person. This is not a simple thing. There are many hurdles that your resume must get over on the typical resume journey, including:

- Upload your resume or attach a hyperlink to your LinkedIn Profile.
- Primary Screening: Resume is run through AI screening software looking for matches to keywords, qualifications, skills, experience.
- Secondary Screening: If your resume makes it through, your resume is revised and screened by an HR screener or recruiter.
- If your resume is selected, you are contacted by HR representative or recruiter for a phone interview.
- Manager Screening: If your interview goes well, your resume will be sent to the hiring manager
- If the manager selects your resume, you will be contacted for an interview.

THERE ARE THREE CRITICAL STAGES IN WHICH YOUR RESUME CAN BE REJECTED

Primary Screening: Complex formatting, hyperlinks, graphics, no match to critical words, no match to the essential background, experience, skills, education, required expertise, certifications, and other exceptions.

GETTING YOUR RESUME TO THE RIGHT PERSON

Secondary Screening: This is the first time a human looks at your resume. They will either like it or hate it, and their job is to weed out resumes. If there are 1,000 applicants for a position and 10% make it through the Applicant Tracking System (ATS), the HR rep doesn't want to interview 100 people, so they will look for ways to select or reject them. Rejection is easy. Spelling, grammar, poor layout, and too wordy or cliché sentences will result in an easy and early denial.

On the other hand, selection can also be easy. You will be different and stand out from the pack if you have interesting experiences, unique roles, personal interests, prestigious schooling or employment history, honors, awards, or hobbies. If you want to be selected, you need to be qualified and different. If rejected, the HR representative will create a second tier (backup) group. If you are chosen, the HR representative will schedule an interview. If you get through this interview, your resume will go to the hiring manager.

Manager Screening: Until now, the person who wants to hire you has not seen any resumes. They get the resumes and interview notes for individuals that make it through to the HR screening. So, remember that out of 350 applications, 35 went to HR, maybe 15 of those were interviewed, and eight made it through that cut. That means that the hiring manager now has eight resumes to look over. Perhaps the hiring manager likes half of those (remember: this person is looking for someone to work both with and for them).

At this point, the hiring manager is trying to get to know the person on the resume and wondering if that person can: 1) do the job well, 2) fit into the culture of the team, and 3) is worth the investment to begin the interview process. The hiring manager may only interview their top three or four candidates, or they may interview none and instead ask to look at another batch of resumes from the second tier.

GETTING HIRED

To make it through this gauntlet of review, your marketing package needs to be effective, convincing, and stand out from the pack. In Chapter Eight, you started developing your package by creating a great sales pitch to sell yourself as a candidate, your Personal Marketing Message. This message contains key messages that you will use to create your resume and cover letters.

Chapter Ten Summary

- Understand the path your resume will take.
- List the places in the resume journey that your past applications have been hung up.
- Develop a plan to get your resume past each screening point.

Chapter Eleven

CREATE A WINNING RESUME

Confining a resume to a single page is good advice for anyone.
– Daniel Lyons

I enjoy rewriting resumes because I highlight strengths in my clients that they don't see themselves. In this section, I will let you see how I write rewrite resumes. There are hundreds of services that will write resumes for you, and there are even more sites that have ideas and recommendations on what you should do with your resume. Have a look around and choose the methods that work best for you. I have had great success rewriting resumes for clients, and here is how I do it. Please keep it clean and straightforward, and avoid fancy formatting.

MINIMUM COMPONENTS OF YOUR RESUME

- Name (include significant certifications such as RN or MBA)
- City, State
- Email (no hyperlinks)
- Phone (no hyperlinks)
- Personal Marketing Message (no heading)
- Core Competencies and Skills
- Significant Accomplishments (optional)
- Professional Summary
- Education
- Certifications and Awards
- Technical Skills (optional)
- Personal Interests

Format: Center your name, city, email, and mobile phone number at the top of your resume's first page.

Cautions on Resume Structure

Do not use an inserted header or footer. Instead, add your name, city, email, and phone number at the top of the page. Decrease the top margin so that it looks balanced. Headers and footers make a mess when they go through the ATS system, and you don't want to risk having your resume rejected due to poor formatting.

If your resume is more than one page, write your name, email, and phone at the top left of each page. I use Times New Roman font, bold, and at least a 14 pt. Font size for name, city, email, and phone number. I use Times New Roman font, bold, and at least a 14 pt. Font size for headings (all caps). I use Times New Roman font and at least a 12 point font size for the body. Use your Personal Marketing Message to insert a two to four sentence introduction to who you are. Keep it simple and avoid using exaggerated terms such as "a fantastic team leader," "effective communicator," or "dynamic team builder." Also, don't forget to include the number of years of professional experience. Add up your work experience, intern experience, and volunteer experience if you did actual work.

Core Competencies and Skills

Your resume's first heading will be below your personal marketing message and titled Core Competencies and Skills. In this section, you should accumulate one or two-word phrases that reflect your experience and abilities. Examples of Core Competencies and Skills are Project management, negotiation, financial analysis, graphic design, and inventory control.

One approach is to go through the job description, the job requirements, and the preferred experience of the job that you are applying for. See if you can honestly put any of them in your Core Competencies and Skills section. If you can, use the exact wording used in the job description.

Continue to develop this list by going through all of your professional and educational experiences and selecting those things in which you can consider yourself proficient. Do not put things in this list that you have done once or very few times. You need to demonstrate that you are confidently capable in each of these and back all of them up with real examples.

To make the Core Competencies and Skills fit on the page, use three columns. I recommend that you have no more than fifteen Core Competencies and Skills, which will equal a maximum of five lines.

SIGNIFICANT ACCOMPLISHMENTS

With over ten years' experience in more than one role, you can insert some significant accomplishments. I recommend no more than three bullets, each a maximum of two lines in length that highlight your most notable achievements. Make them specific. Tell a story, and include your role and company (e.g., "As program director at XYG, I delivered $100 million in increased revenue").

Be specific! Don't add vague accomplishments, such as "successfully managed a team of 10 people" or "identified many opportunities for improvement." If you do this right, the hiring manager will want to interview you to learn more about how you "turned around a department with a $15 million annual loss in 6 months," or how you "used statistical analysis and vendor negotiation to reduce supply chain costs by 25%." You want the interviewer to ask for the details.

PROFESSIONAL EXPERIENCE

Enter your professional experience in reverse chronological order, with the most recent first. The format that I follow is Company, City, Job title, and dates all on one line, with dates justified to the right. In the next few lines, include your important responsibilities and achievements. If you have a Significant Accomplishments section, don't repeat the achievement but mention your role.

All achievements and accomplishments should be in the past tense. Even in your current position, you should use the past tense. If you are managing a team – it will become "managed a team" (Unless, of course, you didn't manage a group at any time in the past). Don't get overly detailed; keep things short and to the point. Your goal for these bullets should be one line, each with a maximum of 6 bullet points. If it is getting longer than this, you will lose the reader, so think in headlines, not paragraphs.

If you include volunteer and intern position, provide the position description. You don't need to advertise these roles as a volunteer or intern. You were working, did things, and got experience. If questioned, tell them. If you performed a detailed statistical analysis of the on-time delivery of raw materials to a manufacturing plant that decreased waste or downtime, no one cares if you were a paid employee. What matters is your experience and skill.

EDUCATION

This section is simple. Add your school, major, degree earned, and the year awarded. Do not include the courses you took. If you had significant any extracurricular accomplishments during your university time, include them (e.g., "Team leader of Varsity Tennis Team," "Governor's Fellowship," or "Student Body President."

CERTIFICATIONS AND AWARDS

Add any certifications, awards, or diplomas that you have achieved. Here you can also put any training or any other educational experience.

TECHNICAL SKILLS (OPTIONAL)

If you are in a technical career, you can add any technical skills here, for example, MS Office 365, SQL, SAS, C+, Six-Sigma Black Belt, Lean Six-Sigma, Epic, Lawson, Project Management Professional, etc. Don't clutter this section with well-known skills such as email, excel, word, iPhone, etc.

PERSONAL INTERESTS

Believe it or not, but this section can be a game-changer. The hiring manager has personal interests. I have gotten more interviews because of my interests than because of my experience. Of course, you have to get through the screening before anyone can notice these interests, but this is an important section.

People hire people, not paper; therefore, you should spend a significant amount of time developing your resume and customizing it for each job you apply. Although this might be time-consuming, customizing your resume gives you a better chance of making a great first impression.

REVIEW AND PROOF YOUR RESUME THOROUGHLY

Review, edit and proofread your resume. Spelling, verb agreement, grammar, and punctuation accuracy all count. Have someone review your resume, suggest corrections, and use a grammar checker and spell checker to make sure you are putting your best resume out there. Hiring managers will balk at candidates with errors because it demonstrates a lack of pride and attention to detail. Your resume is YOU on a page.

Example of a Winning Resume

Sarah Jones

Los Angeles, CA

s.jones.456@wow.com

213.213.2131

With almost two years of healthcare industry experience, Sarah is seeking a dynamic career where she can use her analytical skills and strategic approach to help transform healthcare delivery and improve the patient experience. Sarah performs well either individually or as a team member in a high-pressure, fast-paced, deadline-driven environment.

CORE CAPABILITIES AND SKILLS

Data Analysis; Customer Relationship; MS Office 365; Negotiation; Website Development; RFP Development; Problem Solving; Tableau; Database Management; Executive Reporting; SQL; Business Development

PROFESSIONAL EXPERIENCE

Associate Account Representative, Company X, Los Angeles. June 2019-Present
- Managed communications with clients including triaging and client research requests
- Became Customer Relationship Management system (CRM) "Super-User."
- Solely responsible for data integrity and quality of client interaction documentation
- Created and analyzed client utilization reports

Practice Transformation Assistant, California Medical Group. Jan-May 2019
- Supported AMA campaign to reduce physician burnout and improve job satisfaction
- Conducted research to identify methods to enhance physician wellbeing
- Created RFP to address physician burnout
- Developed evaluation criteria to select health systems to conduct research

Business Development Associate, MedCo., St. Louis. Sept 2018-May 2019

- Managed client relations for the professional consulting team
- Optimized development and management of a large-scale Information System
- Synthesized Health System Management theory between external and internal customers
- Executed creative problem solving regarding the architecture, content, and strategy

Medical Clinic Assistant, Mai Khoi Clinic, Saigon, Vietnam   Jan 2018-April 2018

Supervised clinic visits for hundreds of low-income or unemployed Vietnamese

EDUCATION

- General University Calabasas, BS. Health Systems Management   May 2019

CERTIFICATES AND AWARDS

- American College of Healthcare Executives - Student Associate
- Basic Certificate in Quality & Safety
- General University Social Justice Committee - President

PERSONAL INTERESTS

Big game photography, ultra marathons, poetry, violin, app developmentv

Chapter Eleven Summary

- Collect all of the information you need to construct your resume.
- Draft your resume with absolutely no graphics, lines, headers, or footers. Check your formatting for simplicity.
- Review and correct all spelling, grammar, punctuation, or long awkward sentences.
- Draft your new resume and compare it to the Minimum Components list.
- Review and edit for clarity. Review, rewrite, edit, refine your resume - short headlines vs. detailed descriptions.
- Check your document for grammar and punctuation using a tool such as Grammarly.
- Ask a friend to read and comment on your resume.
- Include a Personal Interests section that is short and to the point.
- Customize your resume for every job application.
- Check your spelling.
- Compare your resume to the example resume.

Chapter Twelve

JUST-IN-TIME COVER LETTERS

What you get by achieving your goals is not as important as what you become by achieving your goals. – Zig Ziglar

Your cover letter is your best chance to display your personality and stand out from the crowd. Everyone has a resume, and every resume is full of experience, education, and skills, and all feel the same. A hiring manager gets very little personal information from a resume and may never look carefully at your resume because, for them, a resume just ticks a box. The cover letter, however, is a quick way to introduce who you are. What is your backstory? What have you really done?

Use your cover letter when applying for any specific role or when you want to connect with a particular person or company. Just like your resume, customize your message to suit each job and each company. Experienced hiring managers can easily spot a generic letter, which starts you off on the wrong foot.

Your cover letter should be concise, less than a page long, and simple to read. The cover letter should provide something that expands on what is found in your resume. The content needs to go into more depth than your title, work history, responsibilities, and accomplishments. It should also dig into HOW you achieved greatness and what that says about your personality.

The letter should be upbeat and genuine and end with a request for a meeting, consideration, further discussion, next steps, a chat, or anything else appropriate to the circumstances. Most of all, your expertise must link to the specific requirements of each job. Customizing your cover letter for each job application can be a daunting task, but the effort is worth it. This step-by-step guide shows you how to assemble your cover letter in a practical yet painless manner by creating all of the components ahead of time and then choosing and assembling the appropriate pieces when needed. This is Just-in-Time cover letter creation.

STEP 1: CREATE YOUR INTRODUCTION SENTENCES

Draft a few versions of simple, to the point introductory sentences. Some may be very brief, others more casual, and others more to the point. All of your introductory sentences should provide the following information: Who you are, what role you are applying for, what specific talent you have to offer, and a statement showing that you are excited (use a word that suits you) about being considered for this position. In a single sentence, make it very clear why you are qualified for the role. Whether you use your name to introduce yourself is up to you, but it is not required because your name is at the top of the page. Refine your introduction sentences often to get them right and reduce the word count. The goal is that your cover letter is no more than a full page in full length and a quick read.

STEP 2: YOUR BACKSTORIES

Of all of the work that you will do to prepare to get hired, this section, Your Backstories, is perhaps the most important and valuable. If you do these correctly, and continue to refine and add to your stories, you will have more powerful ability to communicate who you are to any prospective employer.

You are the sum of your stories. As Keith Richards once said, *"Everybody has a different way of telling a story, and a different story to tell."* Before writing resumes, cover letters, or personal marketing messages, you need to start collecting success stories. These are your stories, and they provide color commentary for your experience.

When you say that you are a *"dynamic leader,"* the reader thinks, *"Don't tell me, show me."* Your story should be an example of what you did that qualifies you as a *"dynamic leader."* People remember stories, and your goal is to be remembered.

Start by making a list of events, hurdles, wins, failures, disappointments, and learnings that make up your professional life. For each of those on the list, draft a short, one-paragraph backstory about those experiences. Use this simple structure for each paragraph: Describe the situation before you became involved, describe your specific actions, and summarize the results of your involvement.

Each backstory should demonstrate one of your key strengths. For example, when asked to describe their experience as a team builder, one of my clients responded, *"At General Inc., I inherited a team of engineers who had not been managed in the past and had failed to deliver on their project goals. I worked with each person to understand their goals, roles, and needs. In team meetings, I helped them choose their most important goal: to change the manufacturing process to reduce product waste by 10%. The team identified how each one would participate. I followed up with the team regularly and helped them get the resources they needed to succeed. Two months later, they met one of their most elusive goals and delivered an 18% reduction in waste."* This answer was a much more detailed description of their team building strength than *"team builder"* and made for a great backstory.

Aim to collect as many of these backstories as possible, with each story focused on your most significant experiences. These events are the most important and useful in illustrating who you are. These are your stories that will make writing your resume, cover letter, and personal marketing message much more manageable. Throughout your career, you will continue to collect and refine your collection of stories.

When writing any cover letter, you should review your backstories. Select two or three stories relevant to the specific job/career for which you are applying. These stories will make writing your cover letter much more manageable.

STEP 3: SELECT YOUR BEST TRAITS

Make a list of two or three of your most important traits or skills that may be helpful in the role. Describe each trait and how that trait has helped you be successful in your career or personal life.

STEP 4: RESEARCH THE SPECIFIC ROLE AND COMPANY

Research and write one concise sentence for each of the following:

The role: Why does this role interest you? (Answer A)

The company: Why does this company interest you? Don't tell them about their own company and avoid statements that may sound like hollow flattery. Be genuine! (Answer B)

Your fit for the role and the company: How does your experience relate to the job? Select the top requirement. How does your experience match? For example, consider the following statement about managing credit risk: "I was responsible for risk management in the credit department for four years." (Answer C)

STEP 5: DRAFT A POWERFUL CLOSING SENTENCE

Draft a simple conclusion sentence. State that you are excited to apply and look forward to advancing through the process or are looking forward to hearing about the next steps.

STEP 6: ASSEMBLE A DRAFT OF YOUR COVER LETTER

Your cover letter is now ready to be assembled. Note that many components can be recycled to minimize any new work to create the cover letter.

- Date
- Company Details
- Salutation: Dear Hiring Manager (do some research to get the right name)
- Your introduction sentences
- Sentence 1: Answer A
- Sentence 2: Answer B
- Sentence 3: Answer C
- Sentence 4: One story from your list of backstories
- Skills/Traits: Bullet Points for Skills or Traits Explanations
- Sentence 5: Your value statement from your PMM
- Close: Always end your cover letters with a Thank you
- Name
- Mobile
- Email

Step 7: Review, Edit, and Revise

Review, review, review. Spell check, read out loud, have someone else read it to you. Review your letter with Grammarly. Grammarly is a tool that checks spelling, punctuation, and grammar, while also providing suggested solutions. If you don't have it, get Grammarly.

When you are satisfied that even the most critical person would not find a single error, save your cover letter as a PDF. Before you press send, review your PDF letter for mistakes or problems that may have occurred when the document was exported to PDF format.

AN EXAMPLE OF A WINNING COVER LETTER

Dear Hiring Manager:

I have always known that a dynamic career in transforming healthcare and the patient experience is fulfilling. A BS in Management and my previous experience put me in a position to be successful as a Healthcare Consultant at Company X.

My roles at the General Medicine and National Medical dealt with disrupting the systemic inefficiencies of physician burnout and chronic care management across health systems, respectively. At General Medicine, I witnessed system-level dysfunction that hinders physicians' ability to provide high-quality patient care. In response, I facilitated efforts to raise awareness, advance knowledge, and catalyze change to reduce burnout and improve professional outcomes.

Through these experiences, I learned how exciting the process of identifying an issue, solving the problem, and increasing value to the intended stakeholder. I want to continue on this path and be at the forefront of further impact.

Professionally, I have four vital traits and skills that I can contribute to Company X:

- A lifetime commitment to learning: at Z Consulting, I was regularly exposed to our clients' projects and what influenced their priorities. I make it a point to stay on top of healthcare trends and initiatives. However, I know a hands-on learning approach will accelerate this learning.

- Quantitative analysis skills: in my current role, I create utilization reports and use intermediate level excel functions to analyze data. Additionally, I can assess datasets to aid decision making.

- Creative expression: healthcare is evolving, and there is a greater need for creative, innovative, and strategic problem-solving. I am experienced in translating data to something visually pleasing, creating websites, and thinking outside the box regarding problem-solving.

- Interpersonal skills: I possess practical written and verbal communication skills. I can collaborate with and influence internal and external partners. The opportunity to work with others efficiently in a high-pressure, fast-paced, deadline-driven environment is captivating.

I believe that my vision and values, professional experiences and skill-sets, and substantial academic achievement align with its brand. I will be a great fit and asset to the organization as a Healthcare Consultant.

Sincerely,

Name

Chapter Twelve Summary

- Write your backstories. The more backstories you have, the better.
- Collect all of the components of your cover letter.
- Assemble your cover letter, proofread it thoroughly and personalize it every time you apply.
- Use your background research and your Personal Marketing Message.
- Spell check often.
- Run your letter through Grammarly.
- Compare your letter with the example cover letter.
- Personalized your cover letter for each job for which you apply.
- Ask a friend to read your cover letter out loud to you.
- Continue to collect your backstories.

Chapter Thirteen

CREATE A WINNING LINKEDIN PROFILE

I spend three hours a day working on my social network profiles. I think about the right people to tag, the ones who might generate new leads. It's my work, my self-promotion. – Maye Musk

Your LinkedIn profile is an essential part of your Personal Marketing Package. LinkedIn is a very useful tool for changing careers, getting a new job, or getting your first job. LinkedIn has almost 600 million members, and about half of them are active users who access the platform daily. Use LinkedIn.

For you to have an effective presence, you need to configure your LinkedIn appropriately. These 38 steps are an essential guide and describe the basics of getting your profile right.

Review your profile weekly. Look for ways to improve and enhance your visibility.

38 Steps to Setting up a Winning LinkedIn Profile

1. Decide on your Selected Career Path (SCP) - (see the "What are Your Options" Section).
2. Update your resume to match SCP - (see Resume section).
3. Craft a generic cover letter to match SCP - (see the Goal Section).
4. Develop your Personal Marketing Message.
5. Update LinkedIn "About" section using a blend of your elevator pitch, cover letter, and resume.
6. Update your profile headline to match SCP and make sure to check the box to "show education."
7. Upload your new resume.

GETTING HIRED

8. Connect with people.
9. Connect with groups that are relevant to you and your career. Pay attention to the group size and choose groups that are large (>1,000 members).
10. Make sure you have included a Job Preferences section.
11. Make sure you have added an Experience section.
12. Under "Me" – Settings and Privacy – Review your privacy settings (Recommended Settings are shown in bold italics).
13. Choose who can see your email address – *Everyone*.
14. Who can see your connections – *Connections*.
15. Who can see your last name – *Everyone*.
16. Choose how you want your name to appear on LinkedIn.
17. Choose how your profile appears via partners' and other permitted services.
18. Choose whether work experience descriptions from your LinkedIn profile can be shown in Resume Assistant, a feature within Microsoft Word – *Yes*.
19. Choose whether you're visible or viewing in private mode.
20. Choose who can see when you are on LinkedIn – *Everyone*.
21. Share job changes, education changes, and work anniversaries from profile – *Everyone*.
22. Notifying connections when you're in the news – *Yes*.
23. Choose whether LinkedIn notifies people in your network that you've been mentioned in an article or blog post – *Yes*.
24. Mentions or tags by others – *Yes*.
25. Choose whether other members can mention or tag you – *Yes*.
26. Choose who can discover your profile if they are not connected to you but have your email address – *Everyone*.

CREATE A WINNING LINKEDIN PROFILE

27. Choose who can find your profile if they have your phone number – Everyone.
28. Choose whether LinkedIn can use public data to help you improve your profile – Yes.
29. Manage or sync contacts to connect with people you know directly from your address book – Yes.
30. Manage or sync calendars to get timely updates about who you'll be meeting with.
31. Choose what information LinkedIn saves when you submit a job application.
32. Let recruiters know you're open to opportunities – Yes.
33. Share that you're free and appear in recruiter searches matching your career interests – Yes.
34. Signal your interest to recruiters at companies you have created job alerts for – Yes.
35. Choose if you want to share your full profile with the job poster when you're taken off LinkedIn after clicking apply – Yes.
36. Stored job applicant accounts – Yes.
37. Manage which third party job applicant accounts are stored on LinkedIn – Yes.
38. Choose who can follow you and see your public updates – All.

With LinkedIn you can expand your network of professional connections, communicate with experts in your chosen field, search for job openings, get yourself known to recruiters, and help others with their careers. Set a target of at least 200 more people to connect with and rapidly expand to beyond 500 connections.

GETTING HIRED

Review your LinkedIn profile frequently. Like and share other people's posts that you read and like, and comment on other people's posts. Be respectful, and kind - everyone can see your content (all social media). If you are rude, insensitive, sarcastic, or overly critical, you will be judged. You won't know the impact until it is too late.

Make sure that you have a professional LinkedIn profile and get connected with people. To complete your Personal Marketing Package, you need to make sure that all of the components: resume, cover letter, personal marketing message, and LinkedIn profile are aligned and consistent.

CREATE A WINNING LINKEDIN PROFILE

Chapter Thirteen Summary

- Review your LinkedIn Profile and compare your profile to profiles of people with job titles similar to or above the title you are looking for.
- Complete all of the 38 improvement steps.
- Review your profile weekly and make continual improvements.
- Send a personal message to everyone you request to connect with.
- Look for other people on LinkedIn that you respect and review their profile - make more changes to your profile.
- Like posts that you read and add a comment - target 5 per day - quality over quantity.
- Keep your resume link up to date.
- Explore your contacts and their connections.
- Reach out to your connections to ask for help, advice, or other connections.
- Use the Career Advice option.

THE GETTING HIRED PROGRAM

PHASE 4 - LAUNCH

LAUNCHING A JOB SEARCH CAMPAIGN

Chapter Fourteen

PLAN YOUR JOB SEARCH CAMPAIGN

In preparing for battle I have always found that plans are useless, but planning is indispensable. – Dwight D. Eisenhower

All the intense preparation that you have done to this point will help your next step; planning and executing your job search campaign. Your campaign requires that you put all of your knowledge and your networking skills into action and use your Personal Marketing Package to get hired.

There is a wealth of information available that is related to project planning. Consult the Project Management Book of Knowledge (PMBOK) for everything related to projects. While I will not burden you with a recitation of project management methods, the following is an outline of just a few components to put into your job search campaign.

MINIMUM COMPONENTS OF A JOB SEARCH CAMPAIGN

- Statement of your ultimate goal and short-term goals, including timeline – you should have one set of goals for your Networking campaign and another for your online campaign.
- Plan B – what will you change if your campaign is floundering?
- Campaign evaluation.
- List of tasks to measure your network campaign.
- Create a detailed list of all network connections.
- Number of new network connections.
- Number of total LinkedIn connections.
- Number of interviews for information.

GETTING HIRED

- Number of communications with existing network connections.
- Number of new jobs identified.
- Number of jobs applied.
- Number of job interviews.
- Number of job offers.
- Number of rejections.
- List of tasks to measure your online campaign.
- Number of new jobs you identified.
- Number of jobs researched.
- Number of jobs applied.
- Number of job interviews.
- Number of job offers.
- Number of rejections.
- Timeline: daily, weekly, and monthly goals for each of the above.

CREATE A JOB APPLICATION ROUTINE, INCLUDING:

- Specific job and company research.
- Update your marketing materials by customizing your resume and cover letter.
- Investigating possible networking connections.
- Weekly summary of progress and tracking all measures.
- Job interview preparation.
- List of decision points – when will you re-evaluate and consider plan B?
- What additional skills, experiences, or competencies do you need to meet your career objective, and what is your plan to acquire them?

Chapter Fourteen Summary

- Review the Project Management Book of Knowledge (PMBOK) with your focus on the planning sections.
- Complete all of the Minimum Components of a Job Search Campaign for an online campaign.
- Modify your online plan for a job search augmented by networking.
- Do the work that you have identified in your plan.

Chapter Fifteen

ACCELERATE YOUR NETWORKING

Being valuable and useful is all you ever need to do to sell things. Help people out. Send interesting posts. Write birthday cards. Record videos sharing your ideas for growing their business. Introduce people who would benefit from knowing each other, then get out of the way, expecting nothing in return. Do this consistently and authentically. – Colin Dowling, Entrepreneur

People with an inside track fill most job openings. People who are less qualified than you but who are well connected to the people who can hire will be more likely to get the job. How do you get to know these people who have or know of the job openings? How do you find and develop quality connections and build lifelong reciprocal relationships? You must aggressively and consistently cultivate and grow your network through viral networking.

Remember the movie Six Degrees of Separation? One of the characters says, "I read somewhere that everybody on this planet is separated by only six other people. Six degrees of separation between us and everyone else on this planet. The President of the United States, a gondolier in Venice, just fill in the names. I find it a) extremely comforting that we're so close, and b) like Chinese water torture that we're so close because you have to find the right six people to make the right connection... I am bound to everyone on this planet by a trail of six people" (Six Degrees of Separation. 1993. [Film]. Fred Schepici, director. USA, MGM).

The hypothesis is that everyone has some connection to anyone in the world through six links, the network. In other words, you know someone who knows someone, who knows someone, who knows someone, who knows someone, who knows someone, who knows Brad

Pitt.

Try it for yourself. Pick a person with whom you would like to be in touch. Now, using your current network, Google search, and LinkedIn, work forwards and backward to see how many people you would have to know to be in contact with that person. Doing this doesn't mean that they will have drinks with you or go to dinner, but you will find a connection.

If you can find the links, try to get a simple phone conversation with that person using the links to introduce you. Focus on quality over quantity and relationships over applications. A meaningful professional relationship can last a lifetime, while an application can be over and done within minutes.

Someone Has a Job Just for You

There is a person who has a job that is a perfect fit for your career. The problem is that you don't know that person with the job. That person is most likely NOT in your network. So how do you get the job? You don't know whom you are trying to connect with, so you don't know who has the job; therefore, you have to network to find the person with the job, and you do this by networking. We have all had this drummed into our heads, and for a good reason. Who has a job is known to someone, and they know someone, who knows someone, who knows someone, who knows you. So you have to bring that person with the job into your network.

Viral networking can create rapid expansion of your contacts. If you start with two contacts and each of these gives you two contacts, and this continues each day, you will have over 1,000 new connections at the end of nine days. When it comes to your success in getting the role that you want and furthering your career, the people who know you are more critical than those you know.

ACCELERATE YOUR NETWORKING

Don't confuse networking with "sucking up." You have to be genuine and be able to deliver the goods. The stronger the relationship you build with each person, the better. Viral networking will rapidly expand the number of connections you have when you have a clear message (PMM) and something to offer, some means of reciprocating. To have something to offer, you need to be prepared, and you need to care about the person genuinely. If you can provide something of value to every connection you make, networking will help others value you and know how well you perform.

Opportunities to network are everywhere. Your inner circle is your family and your close friends, followed by your university or other school connections, military colleagues (if you served), and sports and club connections. The next level comprises professional or work relationships. All contacts are not equal. Some relationships will be willing and able to help you, and you will be willing and able to help some contacts. To work effectively over the length of your career, networking must be a two-way street. If you first think about how you can help a person, you have a higher possibility of forging a meaningful professional relationship. What do you have to offer? Do you have an insight, an article, a book, some knowledge, an idea, or a methodology that might be valuable to share with the person? What do you have to offer?

SOME SIMPLE STRATEGIES TO LEVERAGE LINKEDIN

Who is in your network? This should be your starting point for all networking strategies. Remember that it is easier to develop a meaningful network when working than when you are looking for a job. Create an Excel list of your network and their contact details. Include a note to identify where you met them. Before you apply for any job online, consider these networking strategies using LinkedIn and research to improve your chances of having your resume getting to the right person.

GETTING HIRED

Strategy 1: Who do you already know?

Once you have found some positions that appeal to you, start a list of companies hiring them. Go to the company website and do a more detailed search in their jobs or career section. Then, go to your LinkedIn search for the company and look at people. Do any of your alumni work there? If you have any connections in that company, reach out to them and ask to chat and get their advice on how best to apply. If you don't have links, find a few people who would most likely be hiring managers and ask to connect *"I'm interested in X company and would like to connect."*

Strategy 2: Find out who is who?

Use a combination of LinkedIn and the company website to find out who is the head of HR and who is the head of the department responsible for hiring. You have to do some digging and when you have the names and contact information, reach out to them and ask for their advice concerning how to best apply for the position. Craft these emails very carefully and add some of your PMM into the note. Don't send your resume yet. Ask for permission. Ask to connect. Be interested in what they have posted, and learn.

Strategy 3: Ask your connections for connections

Reach out to your current LinkedIn contacts and ask if they know of anyone at that company. If you can't find anyone in your network, you may want to expand your connections by going to Contacts and requesting to connect with others. A base of 500 contacts will give you a broader network from which to look for help.

Send an email or a LinkedIn message to everyone in your connections and let them know that you are available. Include what type of work you have been doing and ask each of them if they know of anyone you could connect with to discuss your search. See the Interview for Information section for how and why to request a call.

Strategy 4: Find the recruiter to get to the hiring manager

You can sometimes benefit by identifying a recruiter dedicated to a specific company or industry. On LinkedIn, search for the company with recruiter added (e.g., company recruiter), and ask to connect with all of them. If you get a response from the recruiter, tell them that you are interested in a specific job and ask them what they would recommend doing to get your resume into the right hands. They may offer to do this for you, but you should still focus on understanding more about the company and who is who. Do this only after you have applied directly through the company website and gotten no result.

LEVERAGE MEETINGS AND CONFERENCES

Is there anyone else that hates going to conferences? Everyone talks about going to groups, conferences, trade shows, gatherings, or meetings to network. My personal experience with this type of networking has been abysmal. Everyone at these events is interested in one thing, selling. They smile and hand you their card or exchange details, and they hope you may, at some time, buy something from them. At the least, they hope you will tell someone who might buy something.

Why are you there? Did your company tell you to go? Is everyone else going? Do you have FOMO (Fear of Missing Out)? Are you there to sell yourself?

So, there are many sellers and few buyers. Suppose an executive decides to buy a billion-dollar information system for their hospital-based on their attendance at a trade show, conference, or seminar. In that case, their company has a much bigger problem than not having the best technology.

At these meetings, have a plan. Make it your goal to meet at least one person with a common interest or background. Get to know that person and share ideas. Ensure you have something to share, even if it is as simple as an idea or a contact.

Tap into Your Inner Circle

Leveraging your friends and family is the easiest and most straight forward method of networking. It might surprise you that most of your friends and family have or have had jobs. That means that they know people, and some of those people might know who has a need. Let them know that you are looking for a new role and ask them to spread the word. Whom do they know that you might be able to speak with?

You might be surprised to know that job seekers don't often let their families know what they are looking for. This happens consistently the higher up your position is. For some reason, there is a feeling that having a job is good, while not having a job is terrible. Get over it! You are shopping for your career. Your goal is to find those hidden job openings and the people who know of them. Keeping your family in the loop is particularly important if they live in the same city as you, they are in a similar career field, they have deep university connections, or they are active in their communities.

Other networking opportunities include universities, churches, networking groups, clubs, associations, fraternities, sports groups, and volunteering. When you are not working, get involved, and stay involved. Look for opportunities to volunteer, to participate in activities, and embrace your hobbies and interests.

Chapter Fifteen Summary

- Begin a networking campaign by tapping into your current network. Set a goal to increase your LinkedIn connections by 50% within two weeks.

- Try using the three LinkedIn strategies to get to more contacts within your career field.

- Get involved in groups, meetings, sports, etc. Develop two strategies to make meetings and conferences more useful for you.

- Create an Excel tracking spreadsheet and keep detailed notes.

- Ask everyone with whom you speak if they know of anyone that you can connect with.

- Keep everyone on the lookout for opportunities.

- Help others when and where you can. Help one person a month to connect with someone in your network.

Chapter Sixteen

MINING YOUR NETWORK

If you find it in your heart to care for somebody else, you will have succeeded. – Maya Angelou

If you know more than the next person, you will be more likely to make better choices and perform better. You need information to succeed at anything, and other people often know things you want to know, ask them!

Interviewing for information is a valuable skill that is often ignored by both new and experienced job seekers. The objective of interviewing for information is to learn about the career, understand what it takes to succeed in that career and to expand your network. To be effective, you must be well armed with the best questions and the right frame of mind. Once you have identified people within your network whom you would like to interview, reach out to them and ask for some time to meet. Respect the person's time and manage these interviews to last 30 minutes.

There are a few critical rules that, if broken, will spoil the informational interview, and if you follow the rules, you can achieve pretty astonishing results. Your main objective is to get a greater understanding of a subject or career and expand your network. You may ask yourself, "Why would I want to interview someone for information? I need a job, and I want to talk to people who can make that happen". If you already know a person who will give you a job, then you don't need to do these interviews for information.

However, the chances are that you don't know the right person, or you might not know the right person who has a job that might fit your skills and wants to hire you. So, how do you find that right person or that dream career? That's where interviewing for information can be of great help. To be successful at interviewing for information, you must have a curious mind and not want a job from the person that you are interviewing. These interviews are interviews for details about the career, the industry, or a specific company.

Rules of the Road When Interviewing for Information

The four rules to conduct successful interviews for information are as follows: never ask for a job, have something to give, be curious, and always ask for new connections to expand your knowledge.

Rule 1: Never, ever ask for a job

This may be difficult when you are desperate for a job. Still, your objective here is to learn and expand your network. When interviewing for information, you should clearly state to your contact that your purpose is to learn from them. If you ask if they have a job or even suggest that this person's trust in you may be instantly destroyed. In any relationship, whether personal or business, trust is most likely your most valuable asset. Get it clear in your head that you don't expect this person to have a job for you, and that you are not asking them for a job. This point is so crucial that if you are unable, in the quiet of your mind, to genuinely believe that you do not want a job from this person, then stop. If, however, you are committed to seeing the process through, then continue.

Your introduction can have a statement similar to "Would you be willing to let me interview you for information? I know you don't have a job for me, but I need your help in understanding how to enhance my career." People typically love to help people, especially when the pressure is off of them to deliver something (a job) that they may not have. If you ask for a job and your contact doesn't have one for you, they will feel that they are failing you. Take the pressure off of them and help them feel good about helping you.

Rule 2: Always have something to give

What could you do to benefit them? Do your research, understand what goals they're trying to reach, and then figure out how you can make an impact. Here are a few ideas: 1) Do they have a book? Buy ten copies of the book to share with your friends, and then send the author a note; 2) Are they starting a podcast? ITunes reviews are gold, find ten friends to leave reviews, and let the host know; 3) Do they have goals (of course, they do!)? Introduce them to someone who can help them achieve those goals.; and 4) Have you found something in your research that they might find interesting? Send them the information or article.

If you can think of nothing else to give, then consistently engage with and share their content on LinkedIn in a meaningful way. We all have something to give, and sometimes you just need to get creative. The next time you want to connect with someone, find ways to offer value, lead with that, and be persistent.

Rule 3. Be Curious

Be curious and seek understanding. "I would like to understand what XXXX career is like and what I might do to succeed." People are drawn to people who are interested in them. Get them talking about themselves and their journey. With no need to produce a job or come up with an explanation of why they don't have one (making you and her/him feel bad), you are allowing them to do something good for you (making you and her/him feel good).

Research has shown that when people feel good, have fun, and the pressure is off, they are more creative. They are problem-solving both for you and with you. Moreover, they are asking themselves, "Where might you look for opportunities? Whom might you talk to? What might you need to do next?" Listen carefully! Learn! Take notes! You are speaking with a person who is occupying a job that you aspire to have. Their experience can help you navigate and enhance your search.

Rule 4: Ask Whom Else You Might Speak With

After you have spent time learning, you can wrap up with a simple request. "Do you know of anyone with whom I could speak who might speak with further or might be looking for a person with my skills?" This can grow your network exponentially. This is viral networking. If you get valuable information about your desired career and get two meaningful referrals to others you can speak to; your interview will succeed. If you are uncomfortable about asking for this, you can always close by saying, "Thank you for your time and sharing your experience with me. Do you have any recommended next actions for me or anyone who might be helpful for me to speak with?"

Sometimes, if your timing is excellent and you are very qualified, the contact may have a job that they were unwilling to offer up at the beginning. They may be hiring and can put you in touch with the hiring manager or someone inside their organization who needs someone like you. In rare cases, they may design a job just for you. NEVER go into these interviews for information with the intention of getting a job offer. No one reacts well to being played or deceived.

SOME QUESTIONS TO ASK IN INTERVIEWS FOR INFORMATION

- How did you get your first job in this career?
- How long have you been doing this?
- Where did you work before here?
- What did you do to prepare for this?
- Aside from the company you are with now, what are the top firms?
- Why did you choose this career?
- What made you choose this firm?
- To what or whom do you credit your success?
- If you had to do it all again, what would you do differently?
- What are the essential skills I need to be successful?

- What is your typical day like?
- What do you least like about this career?
- What do you most like about this career?
- What is your next career move?
- What advice would you give me as I enter this career?
- What advice would you give me as I look for my next move?
- Who were the most influential people in helping you break into this career?
- What is it about the work that makes it exciting?
- What frustrates you or causes you the most stress daily?
- What are the hours?
- How's the work-life balance?

Listen Carefully and Learn

Listen carefully, and if you don't understand, ask, "Can you tell me more about that?" "I would like to know more about that," or "I'm not sure I fully understand, can you explain a little further?" Never assume that you truly understand what this person has told you. Occasionally, pause, say something like, "So, let's see if I have this right," and summarize in your own words, asking, "Did I get that right?"; "What else can you tell me?" and, of course, the most useful question, "Tell me more about that."

These interviews should be fun and stress-free. Enjoy the opportunity to learn as much as you can about the person and their journey in a career that you are interested in. Bring something to the table (not physically). Offer them something, a contact, an idea, research, an interesting and relevant article. Give to Get!

The more interviews for information that you do, the more you learn, the better you will become at navigating your career. At this point, it is worth giving a final word of caution. After a couple of interviews, you will have a deeper understanding of the profession and be tempted to just nod in agreement.

DON'T GET LAZY!

Prepare your own set of follow up questions to get a more in-depth understanding. Each person you speak with will have a different perspective to help you learn, understand, and expand your network.

Chapter Sixteen Summary

- Practice Interviewing for Information on a friend or colleague and get some feedback.
- Identify two people in your network to Interview for Information and get at least two new contacts from each of them.
- Follow the four rules of Interviewing for Information every time.
- Interview for information as much as you can.
- Meet on their turf.
- Always have something to offer even if it is just a network connection.
- Always ask for other connections to interview.
- Never ask for a job.
- Be curious.
- Be prepared, be interested and interesting.
- Ask before you take notes (not on your computer).
- Listen actively.
- Transcribe, refine and augment your notes in a document after the meeting.

Chapter Seventeen

LAUNCH YOUR CAMPAIGN

The beginning is the most essential part of the work. – Plato

You have created your job search campaign for both applying online and networking. After selecting a career path to focus on, to get a job, you now need to find job openings. Your search must identify the specific job titles, companies that are hiring, and locations with opportunities. In all of your searches, focus on quality over quantity and relationships over applications. A meaningful professional relationship can last a lifetime, while an application can be over and done within minutes.

Get Ready to Apply Online

Applying online can be frustrating, but you can get offers this way. And here's how! As previously mentioned, review your search results and adjust your searches using different variations of the same job title, or perhaps synonyms of the keywords. (project manager, project leader, project director, program manager, team leader, engagement manager, etc.)

Once you find positions that appeal to you, make a list of companies hiring those positions and recruiters who may be trying to fill an opening. If you don't have a company profile that you created during your research, create one.

At this point, time is of the essence. The earlier you apply to a new position, the greater the chance that you will not be screened out simply because they already have filled the position or received sufficient qualified applications.

Even though you are applying online, you can change this opportunity into a networking search to enhance your chances of success. A search for the company on LinkedIn will provide some helpful information. Link yourself to the company by following them. Search for any people from your university who work there, connect with them. For the people that work there, connect with a few of them and ask what they might know about the role or whom they might know who would answer a few questions. In the jobs tab, you can search for job titles, turn on the alert. Next, look for a job being actively recruited for at that company and get ready to apply.

Go to the company website and do a more detailed search in their company jobs or career section. Most career sections or "Work with Us" sections will have a person to contact. Before you contact that person by email, you need to do more research. Look that person up on Google and LinkedIn to understand who they are and determine if they are still working for the company. Get to know as much as you can about the company and where they fit within their industry.

If you are applying using a network connection, you will probably be asked to apply to the position online. Ensure that you send your resume and your cover letter to your contact and respectfully request that they give your materials to the hiring manager.

Customize Your Marketing Materials

Before you apply, customize your resume to highlight the skills, requirements, and experience to match the job listing wording. Only include those attributes that you can substantiate with your training and experience. Do the following to identify the exact words in the job description:

1. Copy the text from the job announcement into a blank MS Word document.

2. Select any requirement description, duties, or expectations and copy these on to a blank page. Recommended descriptions include self-starter, self-motivated, intellectually curious, research and develop sound hypotheses, project management, build presentations, develop work products, and highly motivated individuals.
3. Make a list of the terms most commonly used in the posting.
4. Choose all terms that you can legitimately defend with your experience.

This exercise can be very time consuming but is well worth the effort if you want your resume to get through the Artificial Intelligence resume screening systems. Include these terms in both your resume and your cover letter.

The idea of the cover letter is to help the hiring manager see evidence of your "strong leadership" qualities or your "team builder" and "collaborative" nature. If you claim to be a collaborative person, use one of your stories that you developed in the "Know Yourself" section to demonstrate how you collaborated. Refer back to the cover letter advice to make sure you get it right.

Avoid telling them how good they are, they already know. Also, avoid going into details that are obvious in your resume, they already have them. Keep your cover letter to one page and focus on who you are as a person and what you can do for them.

TAKE YOUR TIME TO SUBMIT YOUR BEST APPLICATION

When you apply for a position, take your time to ensure that your application is complete and accurate. Your application is a legal document. Aside from failing to submit a complete application, the number one thing that can cause you to be rejected at any stage of the application process is lying. Obvious? Maybe not! I have seen applications that have exaggerated employment experience, left out specific jobs, or misstated education or skills. Something as simple as

"Expert in Excel" when the candidate only knew the basics was enough to put their entire application in doubt. So, a word to the wise, err on the side of brutal honesty. As an applicant, you will be screened, checked, tested, interviewed, and tested again.

Companies invest thousands in hiring and training employees. Just like you will pursue your career with careful research and preparation, employers will do the same. The risk-reward for companies is heavily weighted towards the risk side. The upside is that the company hires a great team member who delivers exceptional value. The downside for the company is that once the employee is hired and subsequently fails or is dishonest, its investment is lost. Time and productivity are lost, team morale may be damaged, and in extreme circumstances, such as Arthur Andersen, the entire company and tens of thousands of individuals are out of business, out of a job, and out of luck.

So, take your application very seriously. Be complete and factual. Do not leave a question unanswered. At the least, indicate "Does not Apply" rather than leaving a blank. Assure that your educational history and your work history are accurate.

KEEP TRACK OF EVERYTHING YOU DO

Keep a detailed Excel spreadsheet for all of your job search activities. Record the company, jobs, applications, and contact details of your progress. Use the following Excel Column Headings:

- Company
- Job title
- Date Applied
- Job platform or application (indeed, etc.)
- Person you contacted
- Response
- Date of Response

LAUNCH YOUR CAMPAIGN

- Follow up actions
- Version data of resume and cover letter

Keep extensive notes on all of your job application activities.

To receive my Job Search Excel template, send me an emailing me at info@paulmcblaine.com.

Chapter Seventeen Summary

- Find jobs online that meet all of your criteria.
- Research the job, the company, the people, the leadership.
- Customize all of your application materials, every time.
- Only apply when you can make the time to submit a perfect application.
- Keep complete and extensive records of everything that you do in a spreadsheet.
- Request my Job Search Excel template by sending a message to info@paulmcblaine.com.

Chapter Eighteen

WORKING WITH RECRUITERS AND HEADHUNTERS

Those are my opinions, and if you don't like them... well, I have others.
– Groucho Marx

Many colleagues that I have spoken with have struggled with recruiters. One of my clients said, "The toughest part of modern job hunting is finding a headhunter that works in a transparent and forthright manner. I have had several opportunities that seemed promising evaporate at the last minute. On at least two occasions, I have had the headhunter go radio silent towards the end of the process. I would say that I feel something like a commodity being traded. We are more dependent than ever on headhunters, so I would say that navigating the headhunter jungle has been my biggest challenge over the last several years."

Outside recruiters (headhunters or recruiters that are not employees of the company) get paid if you get hired and stay employed. They are playing the numbers game like you are. Although they might be able to get your resume to the HR representative, that is not as good as getting your resume to the hiring manager on your own or through your network. Knowing a recruiter for a job may help you connect with the HR representative and perhaps a hiring manager, but the recruiter is not a network contact.

USE RECRUITERS WITH YOUR EYES WIDE-OPEN

I have a friend who has been working with a couple of headhunters over the past four years. She has been sent to several interviews all over the country for positions that are an excellent match for her experience and competencies. Still, she has ended up the number two candidate in almost every case. She got the following responses: "We found a candidate that was local.", "We decided to go with someone that we knew." or "We went with an internal candidate."

Without being too cynical, here is what is most likely happening. The headhunter gets paid to put forward candidates. They get paid when their clients are either accepted on a panel of candidates or when their clients get hired. They will have multiple clients that they put forward to boost their chances of success. So, you are competing with the recruiter's other clients.

Add to this that, many times, jobs, particularly those at the middle management level, require that the company or firm have a competitive job search to guarantee an unbiased selection. To subvert this, companies ask recruiters to produce viable candidates that the company can subsequently reject in favor of the candidate that they want. This is not necessarily a waste of time for you. You learn more about the industry and the company, and you have helped the recruiter solve a problem. She/he will be indebted to some degree.

The situation is complicated by cost. Given a choice between an excellent candidate who comes through a recruiter/head hunter or an outstanding candidate that comes directly to the HR representative, the company will almost always choose the direct candidate. The direct candidate costs the company nothing while the recruiter/head-hunted candidate may cost as much as half the candidate's annual salary.

If you want to work with a recruiter, first exhaust your research, aggressively use your network, and apply through the company website. After you have taken these steps, research the recruiter. Ask questions. The recruiter will want to interview you, and you must interview them. Pick their brains before you send a resume to them. Once you send your resume, you may be stuck. Ask questions such as: How do you work with companies? How many clients will be submitted along with my resume? What do you know about the company? Are their internal

WORKING WITH RECRUITERS AND HEADHUNTERS

candidates for this position? How many resumes have you submitted for this position? How does this company hire? Recruiters are not network connections but can be valuable resources of information.

TIPS FOR WORKING WITH RECRUITERS

1. Recruiters are most attentive to the client's need to find a qualified candidate and aren't working to find you a job. They don't start their day trying to find you a job.

2. Recruiters will focus on candidates who are the best fit for the role and candidates who are a better fit than you.

3. Ask the recruiter for the position profile or job description, and discuss with the recruiter the goals and the priorities the hiring company has for filling the position.

4. Ask the recruiter to describe the necessary skills and work history of the ideal candidate and the ideal experiences and talents of their would-be hire.

5. When interacting with the recruiter, listen carefully to understand the question, and clarify, for example, whether the recruiter asks you for your expected salary and what the client's budget is for the role.

6. Before you hang up, set up your next phone call for an update, feedback, time-frames or next steps.

7. Get as much feedback as you can. Ask how your experience and skills compare to that of other candidates. You may or may not get a clear answer, but the information is useful.

8. Recruiters are busy. Write out your questions before any calls, including a list of the points for the recruiter so that you stay in consideration for the role.

9. Don't call recruiters to chat late on a Friday afternoon or first thing Monday morning.

10. Keep your emails and correspondence succinct and brief. Indicate your interest, capabilities, and what questions you may have so that they can address those expeditiously.

CONTINUE TO WORK ALL YOUR STRATEGIES

If you are lucky enough to find a dependable recruiter, don't ignore all of the other work that you need to do. Continue networking! Continue applying! Just make sure that the jobs you apply for don't conflict with the jobs the recruiter is putting you forward for. Nothing worse than two resumes for the same person from different sources. Confusion typically results in rejection.

WORKING WITH RECRUITERS AND HEADHUNTERS

Chapter Eighteen Summary

- List the reasons why you might want to work with a recruiter.
- Review the Tips for Working with Recruiters.
- Write out your list of strategies to make the relationship work to your benefit.
- Make a list of deal-breakers.
- If you can, get a referral to a specific recruiter from a friend or colleague who can vouch for the recruiter's capability and credibility.
- Don't stop your other activities. Stay aggressive.

THE GETTING HIRED PROGRAM

PHASE 5 - WIN

GETTING HIRED

Chapter Nineteen

CRUSH YOUR JOB INTERVIEWS

Strive not to be a success, but rather to be of value. – Albert Einstein

If you crush all of your interviews, you will get hired. All of the interviews that you have during your career are important, but the job interview is your chance to sell yourself. There are several levels of interviews that you may experience. The HR interview, screening interview, video interview, case study interview, a team or panel interview, and the hiring manager interview are the most common.

All of these interviews have one thing in common; preparation is critical. Each type of interview has a different purpose. The screening interview looks for a basic match between you and the job. The team interview looks for a match between you and the team. And by the time you get to the hiring manager interview, you have proven that you have the skills, experience, and work ethic to fit the job. Now, the hiring manager wants to find out if you can deliver, who you are, and if he/she likes you. There is much research that shows that people hire people that they like.

To be ready for each type of interview, do your research, prepare your personal marketing materials, and practice. If you are ready, you only need to be your genuine, confident self. And where does confidence come from? Preparation, experience, and practice.

During the interview, you will also learn more about the company that has requested an interview and maybe your future employer. Remember that you are searching for your next step in your career path, so you need to shop accordingly.

Because you followed the Getting Hired Program, you are better prepared than your competitors. Now is no time to stop. Prepare for your job interviews and get ready to get hired. Dress appropriately, in business attire, as if you were working there already. Be on time.

JOB INTERVIEW PREWORK

First and foremost: Why do you want this position? You need to have thought about this and take the time to consider what leads you to this job. With so many other careers available, why have you chosen this one?

Why is the firm you are interviewing the one you want? Why are they special? I have interviewed many, many people that respond to that question with something like: "I don't really care," or "Aren't they all the same?" or they go completely the other way and say, "Well, you are the best firm on the planet." Be honest and realistic.

The more careful you are when choosing and pursuing a firm, the more they will pay attention to you. People who are interviewing you work there for a reason. The interviewer is typically very proud of where they work and whom they work with. They like their company and want to find people that they like and will enjoy working with. The interviewers will react well to someone who loves their company and respond poorly to someone who doesn't care about their company or career.

Either before or after your interviews at a firm, hang out in their lobby or on-site café. Watch the people going in and out. Who are they, and will you feel good being one of them or working with them? Do some further due diligence. Read about the CEO. Check out who is on the Board of Directors.

Most importantly, Google the company and select news to see the company's latest information. I once walked into an interview only to learn that, two days prior, they had been sold, and everything was changing. They were surprised that I didn't know. I was surprised that I was so careless.

To Win, You Must be Better Prepared Than Your Competition

I can't overemphasize that to be competitive and win, you need to be better prepared and more capable than your competitors. Use the job description in the posting as a guide to identify each of the job descriptions/responsibilities listed and create a one or two-line answer in response to being asked: "How have you done X?" Do the same for each of the job requirements and necessary experience. If you are lacking in an area, think about how you might respond by relating some other experience or skill to do a similar task.

Finally, what is the question that you fear the most? Sooner or later, someone will ask that question, and you need an answer. Even if the question is never asked, the anxiety that the "dreaded question" might be asked will cause unnecessary tension. Get rid of the stress by facing the question head-on and having a great answer up your sleeve. Again, you need to be honest in your responses, but there is no requirement to overshare. You know all of the details, but is the interviewer interested? Think about your answer as an advertisement might be worded, punchy, and focused on making and essential point. What is the point you are trying to make when you answer the "dreaded question?" Avoid making your response sound like the warnings on a pharmaceutical ad.

Common Job Interview Questions

The objective of the interview is to find out "who you are" beyond what is on your resume. People don't hire pieces of paper; they hire people. So, if you are fortunate enough to be selected for an interview, be prepared. There is only one way to answer each of these questions, your way. You will be better prepared if you think about them and prepare how to answer each question. No one will answer the question the way that you do, and your answer demonstrates who you are. Don't memorize, just know your stories, be prepared, and make your objective to convey your personality.

GETTING HIRED

TYPICAL JOB INTERVIEW QUESTIONS

Here are some of the typical topics and questions that you may encounter in an interview:

- Tell me your story. (This is an opening to use your PMM)
- Why do you want to be a XXX?
- Why do you want to work for us?
- What do you know about us?
- Where do you see yourself professionally in 5 years?
- If you don't achieve these goals, what will you do?
- Is there anything you regret? What is it?
- What work experience do you have?
- I feel that you may be overqualified for this position. How can we be sure that you won't be bored and dissatisfied?
- Describe a situation that you struggled with, and how did you fix it?
- What is your approach to working with someone more motivated than you?
- What is your approach to working with someone who is less motivated than you?
- Describe a failure that you have experienced.
- What about your career disappoints you most, and why?
- What has been the biggest disappointment in your life, and how did you handle it?
- How do you deal with all-nighters?
- Describe your best team experience and why it was good.
- Describe your worst team experience.

- And, the always present "What is your weakness" – try not to use the obvious and overused answers, e.g., "I am impatient to get things done, and sometimes I get frustrated that others can't keep up."
- What would you do if your boss gave you more work than you could reasonably handle?
- How do you manage your time when working remotely?
- Give me an example where you struggled with the social isolation of remote work.
- How do you hold yourself accountable and give me a specific example?
- What is the worst mistake you have ever made?
- Give me an example of your self-starting abilities.
- What would you do if you were asked to take a challenging assignment and had to relocate?

Practice Your Responses

Think through these questions and write out your answers for each item. Keep your responses short, about two to three sentences. Write a couple of variations. For the more complex questions like "Describe an instance where you were working on a team, and there was conflict within the group, what did you do to help resolve the conflict?" or "Describe your best experience working on a team and why." You will want to develop a couple of real-world examples to describe how you worked through these. If you haven't had these experiences in a work environment, think of something you can draw upon in your personal life. If you answer a "yes" or "no" question, include in your answer an explanation.

The reason to not simply answer "yes" or "no" is that these closed-ended answers do not provide any information about you or your experience. The interviewer has a mental framework for what they want to know from each candidate. In essence, they have a checklist. Providing a complete answer makes it more difficult to check "No."

For example, you have managed some aspects of a project but did not have the project manager's title. If the interviewer asks, "Have you ever been a project manager?" Your answer should be something like, "I have been fortunate to get the opportunity to control some important deliverables. While working on an IT transformation project, I was responsible for managing the communication plan." In this way, the interviewer learns something about you. If you answered "No," the interviewer learns nothing and they check "NO."

For questions related to your background and experience, if you don't have a work/job-related expertise to share, improvise, generalize, use your experience in school, volunteering, sports, clubs, or church to illustrate your knowledge and experience related to the question. If you can't come up with something, try to use something that you have done in your life and link it to the subject. Answer the question. Not answering or not attempting to answer the question is a death sentence for any job interview.

You Have to Fit into Their Culture

Most companies are looking for excellent people who match their culture. Hire for cultural fit because skills can be taught. Think about it this way: how often do people change their personalities or core behaviors? Not often. So, companies hire people they like and are willing to invest in training and experience.

When challenged on your lack of skill or experience, you could respond, "While I don't have that particular skill, I believe that I am a good cultural fit for your firm, and being a fast learner, I will be able to be effective quickly." You should include an example of where you have had the same challenge and how you succeeded.

Don't duck a question. This is not a good strategy during a job interview. Equally damaging is claiming that you never had an issue, problem, failure, or struggle. Everyone has had failures, and if you haven't failed, you haven't tried. No one is perfect, so don't try to appear as such.

Deceit during an interview is very harmful. The interviewer is not concerned with failure, but rather how you respond to failure. What did you do when you messed up? What did you learn from the experience? Don't over answer. The interviewer asks a question for a reason. Your answer should be crafted to answer the question, but there is no need to be overly specific.

Excessive details cloud your message. "Tell me something about how you manage the start of a project." Excess detail would sound like, "I would sit down with my computer and develop all of the tasks required into an Excel spreadsheet. I would think about the time required for each task, who could do the task, and when the task needs to be completed." While this is precisely what you "MIGHT" do, a better interview answer could be. "After meeting with the project sponsor to find out the key objectives, I would create a project charter, assemble a team, and develop a work plan. Then, I would review all of this with the project sponsor."

Use the list of your life experiences, your backstories. In preparing for the interview, review the life experiences that have significantly impacted who you are and what you are all about.

Breathe! During the interview, you may be tempted to extend your answers in an unconscious attempt to reduce the number of new questions. Don't do this! Interact with the interviewer. Stop occasionally and ask if what you are saying makes sense. Listen to the interviewer's questions, and clarify that information before answering.

GETTING HIRED

CLARIFY WHAT YOU HEARD TO GIVE A BETTER ANSWER

Before you jump in and start answering a question, you can always ask a simple clarifying question. "You asked me about my project experience. Are you interested in a particular example of working on a project or my broader experience as a project manager?" Clarify the information to know precisely what the question is and what they are looking for in your answer. It never hurts to clarify and check-in.

You may get questions about what you do when you are not working or studying. This is an opportunity to find something in common with you and to put you and the interviewer at ease. Interviewing is stressful for both of you. The interviewer wants to get to know you and find out what makes you tick. This works well in reverse if you recognize something that you have in common with the interviewer. Almost any two people can find something in common if you pay attention and listen carefully.

TEN RECOMMENDATIONS FOR JOB INTERVIEWS

A great interviewer will often challenge you on something. My first interview for a consulting job was with the very experienced owner of a boutique firm. He challenged me on my hairstyle and attire. It wasn't that my hair and suit were terrible, but the interviewer, who later became my boss, wanted to see how I would respond to criticism. Trust me, I was not dressed shabbily. I was wearing a black, double-breasted, Italian blazer and tan slacks, and my hair was combed neatly (with some hair spray to make it stay there, I have very fine hair that tends to have a mind of its own). "I think your hair is a little severe, and you are dressed like you might be going to a Hollywood meeting." I took a deep breath. "You know," he continued, "Your first assignment may be on a factory floor working or working with teamsters," I assured him that I had worked in a wide variety of situations and that I was sensitive to appearances. I told him about my Navy days working as an electronics repair person in a foreign country. Bottom line: if you have thin skin and become defensive, you can start looking for somewhere else to interview and work; this might be too challenging an environment for you.

1. PREPARE FOR THE WORST OR MOST DIFFICULT QUESTIONS

What is the question that you fear most? We all have these. You need to be prepared for that question to not startled or put on the spot if you are asked. If there is anything on your resume that might raise a question, prepare to answer it. "Why did you leave your last job?" "What did you do between these two jobs?" "Why were you at job X for only four months?" There is always more than one reason why seemingly bad things happen during a career, but try to focus on positives as much as possible. What did you learn?

Be prepared to answer, "Are you interviewing with any others? Do you have any outstanding offers? Who else are you looking at?" Honest, open answers are best.

2. SOMETIMES THINGS JUST DON'T WORK OUT

Take ownership and responsibility for your current job. If you aren't able to reinvent yourself and turn things around, resign if you think you might be fired. Being fired is hard to explain away. I wouldn't suggest that you won't be able to find a job if you have been fired. However, the competition for open positions is so high that interviewers are focused on rejecting applicants from the sea of qualified or overqualified applicants. Interviewers can more easily understand a resignation, not so much being fired.

After only three months, I once left a job for two reasons: 1) the company hired me to make some dramatic changes, and their executive team was not ready or willing to support me to make those changes. They hired me too early, and 2) I got a better offer for a position that I had interviewed for months prior. So, my departure was a win-win.

GETTING HIRED

3. NEVER CRITICIZE COMPETITORS, COLLEAGUES, OR PAST EMPLOYERS

If you tell a stranger (interviewer) something that you don't like about someone else, they can only assume that you will soon be talking about them to others. Hiring managers want people on their team that are discrete and not gossips or complainers.

4. NEVER LIE, NOT EVEN A WHITE LIE

This may seem obvious, but in the heat of battle, the temptation can be great to stretch the truth. Don't exaggerate. Most interviewers are experienced professionals. They have done more interviews with more candidates than you will ever have job interviews. Most interviewers can spot someone who is blowing things up. Every answer you give is subject to follow-up questions that, should you be caught out by any, could make the interview very uncomfortable. At the same time, don't sell yourself short. Sell hard, but sell what's real.

5. DON'T GET DEFENSIVE

If you are questioned about any of your responses, don't be defensive; instead, seek clarification and answer calmly and sincerely. Interviewers want you to be yourself and get past the nerves. But if you get too casual or flippant, you may talk yourself out of a job. Assume at the beginning that they want to hire you (which is why you got the interview).

6. ASK QUESTIONS AT THE END

Make sure you have thought through some key things you would like to know. Be curious! "If I were lucky enough to get an offer, what would be the likely level?" "Who would I report to?" "How long is the probation period, etc.?" What is my likely career progression? Where would assignments be? Logistics? Benefits? Corporate culture? Remote work?

7. FOCUS ON BENEFITS, NOT SALARY

Many interviewers get a bad taste in their mouths when salary is the first thing out of your mouth. Delay this question until you are well on your way to receiving an offer. Don't forget, however, to ask about total benefits. Most companies think in terms of total benefits because total benefits are what they pay for when they hire someone. Companies pay for healthcare, life, and disability insurance, and they also pay for paid time off, training, and a wide variety of benefits, including salary.

When the time is right, you can always ask the typical starting range that you might expect. Interviewers expect you to ask, and if you never ask, that can be a red flag, but tread lightly. Don't sell yourself short, but don't exaggerate your worth to the firm, by now they know the value you bring to them and what you are worth to them. The time to think and negotiate salary is if and when you receive a formal, written offer of employment.

8. RELAX AND ENJOY THE PROCESS

What is the worst thing that can happen? Seriously, what is the worst thing that can happen, and if that does happen, what is your plan? You must have a plan.

9. BEWARE OF GETTING TOO COMFORTABLE

After you have been in the interview for over 30 minutes, you may find yourself relaxing and open about your answers and body language. CAUTION: The interviewer is interested in you and your story and wants to know you better. Resist the urge to treat them as a buddy, friend, or colleague. Be yourself, but DON'T SAY ANYTHING STUPID. Keep the wisecracking, slang, joking, or being opinionated to yourself. The interviewer wants to see how you relate to people and how you might work with people.

GETTING HIRED

There was once a very bright young man who had all of the qualifications to get the job. He had it in the bag! As he left, the interviewer asked, "So, what are your plans for the weekend?" The young man responded, "I'm going to celebrate (he had yet to be offered the job) and have shots with my friends!" The interviewer was a teetotaler, and needless to say, the young applicant was not offered the job. Be yourself, but don't be silly! Remember that not everyone has your view of the world or your values. People hire people that they like, and many times, people who are like themselves. Strong opinions may seem like a strength, but you need to know whom you are talking to.

And this doesn't stop just because you get hired. Be sensitive to your co-workers and respect them as individuals. I watched interviewees ace the interview and get the job, only to be fired soon after their true nature was exposed. They might lack empathy, tact, sincerity, and courage, or worse, they might not possess all of the competencies and skills that they claimed on their resume.

10. Prepare

Practice, practice, practice. You don't want the job of a lifetime to be your training ground for interviewing. Do mock interviews with friends or a mentor. Video record your practice sessions and review them with a critical eye, and then do it again. Like the Personal Marketing Message, you must deliver your interview with the passion that lets the interviewer know that you are excited about it. Someone less qualified or talented than you will get the offer if they are more enthusiastic about the company and the job. Skills can be taught, but passion cannot!

Finally, Get Immediate Feedback

The best time to get feedback is when you are in front of the interviewer. Ask for feedback. "Do you have any feedback for me?" is the simplest and most straightforward question. The worst thing that can happen is that they have no feedback for you. Then, listen carefully, and ask follow up questions. If the feedback is negative, take it on board and thank them for their honest appraisal. You can ask a follow-up question, such as, "Do you have any suggestions for me?" Again, listen. Do not be defensive. Thank them for their help. If the feedback is positive, ask about the next steps and timing.

Chapter Nineteen Summary

- Do your research. Know the company and the position.
- Be better prepared for your interview than any of your competitors.
- Review the possible interview questions.
- Use the backstories from your background research.
- Know your Personal Marketing Message cold.
- Have some meaty questions to ask.
- Be interested, be interesting.
- Get feedback while you are there.
- Ask about the next steps.
- Send a thank-you note with two or three ideas of what you can contribute to the company.
- Ask for more feedback.

Chapter Twenty

AFTER YOUR INTERVIEW

It is better to start as a fool and learn from your mistakes than to fake being a genius and ignore your errors. – James Clear

After any meeting or interview with a potential employer, you should follow-up with them. This follow-up is another critical opportunity to sell yourself. A prompt reply tells people you are on-time; a well thought through response tells people that you care, and a new idea or thought tells people that you are thinking. A respectful response tells people that you are respectful. Take your time and do these follow up messages properly. Words mean something, especially when written; what you say and how you say it can make a substantial impact.

POST-INTERVIEW FOLLOW-UP

Now that you have had an interview, you know much more about what the company is looking for. Highlight what you have learned with active verbs. For example, "With my five years' experience in cybersecurity, I will be able to reduce fraudulent transactions for the financial risk department." Once again, dig into your backstories for those that are most appropriate to the job, based on the expanded understanding that your interviews have given you. Include two or three in your follow-up note.

Always follow-up by sending a thank you note. An email may be the easiest way to do this, but something tangible like a handwritten note leaves an impression. I recommend you do both; an email immediately after the interview, followed by a physical message sent by snail mail. In your email, always ask if there is any additional feedback, recommendations, or suggestions.

Post Rejection Feedback

Feedback following rejection is crucial. If you don't have a feedback loop that allows you to make changes and adjustments, you end up in a cycle of repetition. Remember that Einstein said, "Doing the same thing repeatedly and expecting different results is the definition of insanity." We are told, "If at first you don't succeed, try, try again." That should read, "Change, and then try again."

If you fancy your chances of being offered a position with this company, you should do some preparatory work. Under what conditions would you accept a position? Write them down. Under what conditions would you reject the job? Write them down. And finally, what are you willing to negotiate?

Psychometric and Other Tests

Before being offered a position, you may be asked to complete some tests. Examples include the competency test, case studies, and, of course, the psychometric test.

To weed out those that might game their interview and application, larger (and increasingly many smaller) organizations require a psychometric test. These tests are a type of personality test that identifies characteristics that may or may not be suitable for the career to which you are applying. Caliper and Hogan Assessments are just two examples of dependable personality psychometric tests. Firms want to ensure that you will mesh well with their culture and their business. These tests may also help identify individuals with behaviors or personalities that are not wanted in the team.

Forget trying to game these tests. You may see a lot of references on Google to gaming psychometric or aptitude tests. You can't possibly know what the company is looking for, so to be a successful candidate and get hired, you need to be yourself. The statistical background for these tests is so refined that gaming or attempting to game the answers can be easily identified. No company wants to hire someone trying to manipulate their personality profile test before they are hired because they will wonder what they are hiding. Be yourself!

The Offer and Negotiation

You get a call from either the HR representative or the hiring manager. "We would like to offer you the position." Your brain goes crazy. Now is not the time to relax. There are still a lot of unanswered questions and a critical decision to make: Yes! or No!

Up until now, the company has been in the driver's seat. Now, it is your turn to be in control, and that has been the goal. You still have work to do. If you have done your follow up work, as mentioned above, you will know your criteria for accepting, rejecting, or negotiating. Under what conditions would you not negotiate?

Companies expect you to negotiate your salary. You can sometimes negotiate your paid time off (PTO), working hours, remote work, and education benefits. It never hurts to ask. Most HR Representatives will site company policy to resist attempts to negotiate these things, but you never know. So, what could they give you that costs them nothing but is of great value to you? A dedicated mentor, a buddy, a company-wide announcement of your joining, or a press release could all be worth asking for. One benefit that is often overlooked is a sign-on bonus. "Do you offer a sign-on bonus?" Again, it never hurts to ask.

Being enthusiastic about the offer is good, but sleep on it before you make a decision. Ask yourself, does this company culture meet my needs? Will I be happy here? Can I be most successful here? How does it feel? If something seems a little off, you probably need to ask some more questions.

GETTING HIRED

Rarely will a company withdraw an offer of employment if you want time to think, ask more questions, or consider other offers. If you genuinely have other offers, let everyone know, but never bluff. If a company suspects that you are bluffing (because they hear "I have other offers" all the time), your negotiation power is diminished. Be open and honest and have a rationale description of why each negotiation area is essential to you and them. Then, decide!

AFTER YOUR INTERVIEW

Chapter Twenty Summary

- Send a thank-you note with a backstory or two that describes how you will add value to the company.
- Ask for feedback.
- If you receive a rejection notice, follow-up is critical. Send a thank you letter and ask for honest feedback.
- If you receive an offer, express excitement and enthusiasm for the offer and ask for time to review, consider, and speak with your family.
- You should have already prepared your "walk-away" point as well as your needs. The walk-away represents the conditions that would cause you to say, "No, thank you." Your walk-away can not be negotiated; otherwise, it is not the bottom line.
- Write down what you want – include everything, not just salary.
- Write down everything that they could give you that would cost them nothing but would be valuable to you– public notice of your hire, inclusion in specific meetings, flexible start times, etc.
- Write down everything that you could give them that would cost you nothing but would be valuable to them – a certification or degree that you will do at your own cost.

Chapter Twenty-One

AFTER YOU ARE HIRED

Starting a new job can be nerve-racking, but it's also exciting. You're embarking on a new future, positioning yourself to write a new story on a clean slate. – Adena Friedman

Congratulations! You have followed the Getting Hired Program of career management. You have done all of your research, networking, job search, applications, interviews, and negotiations, and now you have a job. Celebrate! Relax! Smile! You have cleared the first hurdle.

However, don't get too relaxed. Now, you need to make the best of your good fortune. It would be best if you lived up to all of the promises and claims that you made in your resume, cover letter, and interviews. People have long memories. The hiring manager will remember that you said you were great at building teams, especially when you struggle to get a group together to accomplish a straightforward task. You must live up to your sales pitch.

In every role, you must succeed. An interesting way to approach your role is to think of what headlines you want or need in your resume. If you aspire to an executive position, your resume needs evidence of broad leadership, the ability to motivate teams, the unrelenting pursuit of exceptional results, expertise in your given field, and the list goes on. Redefine your career goals and spend some time updating your career plan.

When I hired new consultants, I told them that getting hired was the easy part. Coming out the other end with a successful career experience or even a solid reference on your resume is the difficult part. This is where the hard work begins. In the Resources section at the end on this book, I have included a checklist for your first hundred days in a new job, role, or company. This will provide you with some ideas to jump-start your career in your new job.

Chapter Twenty-one Summary

- Please send me an email at info@paulmcblaine.com and let me know where you were and when you were hired and request an electronic copy of the First Hundred Days Checklist.
- Develop a plan for your next career move.
- Let everyone know about your new role.
- Thank everyone who helped you, listened to you, believed in you.
- Celebrate your success.
- Update your Personal Marketing Message and your marketing package.
- Continue to expand your network.
- Be successful!

Chapter Twenty-Two

PARTING ADVICE AND FINAL WORDS

Everybody has talent, it's just a matter of moving around until you've discovered what it is. – George Lucas

I leave you with some ideas and recommendations that my clients have found useful. They are certainly not written in stone, but they represent my thoughts based on my personal experience.

- Ask for help. Never be afraid to ask for help.
- People like helping people, they don't like being used.
- Answer and acknowledge every email, text, or phone call promptly for the rest of your career.
- Have something to offer people who help you.
- Remember to say thank you.
- Make it a point to help others in your network.
- Never say "No" to an opportunity before you are offered that opportunity.
- Never say "No" because you think they might say "No."
- If you have a job, make the very most of it before you decide to leave.
- Always have the next step in mind for your career.
- Always be looking; it is easier to get a job when you have a job.
- Shop for companies that you respect and that you want to work for.
- Shop for the people you want to work with or for.
- Don't be afraid to pick up and move.
- Get in the habit of saying "Yes" to opportunities.

GETTING HIRED

- The best opportunities are the ones that no one else wants to do.
- Trust the process and do the work.
- Measure and track all of your activities and progress.
- Be willing to do what no-one else wants to do and then do it well.
- Be willing to work harder than anyone else.
- Working smarter does not excuse you from working harder.
- No job or career is worth destroying yourself or your family.
- Know what your fears are and create options.
- Always have a plan B.
- Be friendly, confident, and prepared.
- Become the best salesperson for you and what you have to offer.

PARTING ADVICE AND FINAL WORDS

FINAL WORDS

While in a management consulting company, I briefly took my focus off of my career. It seemed to me that my mentors and the leadership team were consistently coaxing me into positions of higher authority and greater opportunity. I enjoyed being looked after and the prestige of rapid career advancement. I was doing great work and felt totally in control, until one day, I wasn't. My sponsors wanted to cash out, and unbeknownst to me, arranged to sell the business. I didn't know where to turn. I had gotten out of the habit of driving my career, and now I was forced to sink or swim. It took me 15 months to find my next role, and I vowed there and then that I would never let anyone or any organization be in control of my career. After all, creating my career has been and remains my most important job. Don't short-cut any of the phases.

THE GETTING HIRED PROGRAM PHASES

1. Investigate - Learning and Building Knowledge – so that you are well prepared to make informed decisions.

2. Focus - Making a Meaningful Decision – so that you get the job you want and are capable of doing.

3. Prepare - Creating a Marketing Package – so that you can sell yourself and your talents.

4. Launch - Launching a Job Search Campaign – so that you have a plan to measure your progress and adjust.

5. Win - Getting Hired – so that you can crush your job interview, respond to offers, and get your new job off the starting line.

The Getting Hired Program can help you throughout your career. You will have many job changes during your working-life, and you will continue to be successful if you do the work. With the Getting Hired Program, you have the tools to drive your success. Take charge of your career and create the path that you want. Succeed!

RESOURCES

Thoughts and Suggestions from Colleagues

I have had the good fortune to meet some exceptional people during my career and life. They represent CEOs of Fortune 100 companies, consultants, physicians, research scientists, entrepreneurs, Ph.D. students, V.P.'s, Directors, Managers, and Presidents from a variety of industries and from around the globe. When drafting this book, I surveyed many of them for their advice and recommendations of what I should highlight in this book. I have tried to incorporate them all as best I could. Because I have a deep respect for having great insights and knowledge about what it takes to get hired and be successful, I want to share their thoughts with you, in their voice.

KNOWING YOURSELF

Know how to critically analyze your skillset and match it to job openings so that people don't end up chasing rainbows with no chance of success and a 100% chance of yet another demoralizing rejection.

—

The most important topic I think is self-awareness, confidence and mental health. I think folks that have this mastered really succeed in job interviews and typically land the job.

—

It is hard to fake being happy and positive all the time but knowing that better days are ahead and to never give up.

—

See yourself, the investment in you and your career as an asset. We need to be more intentional, look at our skills both soft and hard and seek out opportunities to progress those for greater effectiveness. We need to shift and see that so many things from work and life have a 40 year return on investment.

GETTING HIRED

My biggest challenges have been being prepared when challenged by being over qualified, too old or too young, or dealing with a general lack of opportunities (but you can't control that).

CHOOSING YOUR CAREER

We have a tendency to apply a jobs that we have the skills and/or experience to do instead of more narrowly (and passionately) focusing on jobs that we want.

—

Folks focus too much on the short term to get the title or pay they want, but they need to have a long term strategic career plan. I've seen too many people take on a new job just for the title or pay, but it doesn't help them to advance in the long term. People also forget that sometime the best job might be a lateral position that provides new skills or leadership opportunities or positions you for a bigger promotion later.

—

Resilience, not quitting as you will get a number of knock backs/rejections. Understanding, accepting and learning from this e.g. how best to get your resume through an A.I. screening process is crucial.

RESUME

Ensure that your resume/experience matches the role, and you are prepared with specific examples of accomplishments to highlight in the resume and interview. If the role requires sales growth, the resume must reflect experience growing sales, including where, how much, statistics and a quick how such as via price restructuring, opening new markets and aligning sales team incentives. The resume is a screening tool, it's the place to show a great fit, rather than excess variety.

THOUGHTS AND SUGGESTIONS FROM COLLEAGUES

Study the role, the job description, the profile of successful individuals in the target company, and then highlight or give more text/space to those key skills and accomplishment. Reference these in a cover letter as well.

Resume uploading with a plain text file to make life easier with all those Taleo or Workday HR software programs for resume intake? (Frankly I really dislike those programs, but understand why the exist, but don't think they're appropriate for an HR department to use for executive roles).

—

Ensure that your resume/experience matches the role, and you are prepared with specific examples of accomplishments to highlight in the resume and interview.

—

Right or wrong, some employers view too much unrelated experience as an indication that the candidate has unrelated passions, distractions, may not be a good fit, or will quit when a different type of opportunity arises.

—

Study the role, the job description, the profile of successful individuals in the target company, and then highlight or give more text/space to those key skills and accomplishment. Reference these in a cover letter as well.

—

Know how to frame your experience and make it relevant to the role but somehow what is the x-factor you bring (given the organizations strategy, the key role outcomes etc.) that is unique to you as a candidate.

—

A demonstration of the ability to work unsupervised is going to be more important. Maybe even the ability to manage a remote workforce is going to be a key skill.

Above all, the candidate needs to be relevant! Does the resume fit my company's and the job's profile? Has the candidate done the necessary research.

—

The game is to figure out what the hirer is looking for. Skill requirements are secondary.

WORKING WITH RECRUITERS

Because I have always been recruited, I really haven't had any challenges getting hired. Staying out of my recruiters' petty battles after being hired is another story!

—

The toughest part of modern job hunting is finding a headhunter that works in a transparent and forthright manner. I have had several opportunities that seemed promising seemingly evaporate at the last minute. It seems to me that we are more dependent than ever on headhunters, so I would say navigating the headhunter jungle has been my biggest challenge over the last several years.

—

Be aware that the headhunter/recruiter essentially works for their client, who is the hiring company, and is not working for the candidate. The recruiter, to be successful, must keep the hiring company's needs and interests above that of the candidate.

—

The client's requirement and headhunter's goal is to present to the client several qualified candidates, some of whom may be more qualified than you. As such, they're much more oriented to the clients needs to find a qualified candidate, and aren't really working to find you a job. If you are a fit, great, but if not, they'll focus on candidates who are a better fit from you. Don't imagine that they are starting out every day trying to find you a job.

THOUGHTS AND SUGGESTIONS FROM COLLEAGUES

As early as possible in the search, get from the recruiter the position profile or job description, and, discuss with the recruiter the goals and the priorities the hiring company has for filling the position.

—

Discuss with the recruiter the necessary skills and work history of the ideal candidate, and the ideal experiences and talents of their would-be hire.

Make sure you understand the questions they ask, and their context. For instance, when the recruiter asks what your expected salary might be, also ask what the client is budgeting as a salary for the role. Likewise for skills, ask what skills the client is ultimately looking for.

—

Your role in the recruitment process may in large part ensure a diverse slate of candidates is presented, even though you aren't the leading candidate. This may feel like a waste of time, but if you're able to participate, you may learn more about your own industry, the competition, and the recruitment process, so it may be worth playing along.

—

Ask how your experience and skills compares to that of other candidates. You may or may not get a clear answer, but the information is useful so that you can strengthen any deficits you may appear to have.

—

Realize that the recruiter is extremely busy, and won't have time to chat all morning about the roll. Have your questions written out before any calls so you're sure to get them answered, and, likewise have a list of the points you want to make to the recruiter so that you remain in consideration for the role. Don't try to call them to chat late on a Friday afternoon or first thing Monday morning.

GETTING HIRED

Networking

Possibly one of the most important chapters might be networking. This is the single biggest fear of most people, and job seekers in particular.

—

I can't overemphasize the importance of forging strong, authentic bonds with people who could later serve as references. For an undergraduate in science, seek to do undergraduate research with a good advisor.

Initiating, building and keeping relationships. Not burning bridges. Carefully establish relationships with quality professionals, even if they are in different areas of the firm.

Know how to use your network. What is the best way to engage people? How to feel like you are not 'using' them. I think you generally need to know someone for senior roles.

—

The biggest challenge in getting hired is getting yourself and/or your documentation in front of the right person.

Job Search

Preparation: Do your homework – get a solid understanding of the company, its objective, its marketplace, its timing cycle (FYE, EOY, etc..) – not just from the website, use LinkedIn and your network to find out as much as you can.

—

My biggest challenge in getting hired is not the interview process, because I am confident through my preparation, but merely getting a recruiter to pick up my resume and getting that initial call. Sometimes even with a referral, you don't get the initial call.

THOUGHTS AND SUGGESTIONS FROM COLLEAGUES

If possible in each conversation, set up the next phone call for an update, either for feedback, timeframes or next steps in the process.

—

Keep emails and correspondence succinct and brief whenever possible. Indicate your interest, capabilities, and what questions you may have so that they can address those expeditiously as well.

JOB INTERVIEW

Spend time preparing for and getting through the phone interview, which is now by and large either a video answering pre recorded questions or a zoom type meeting, they can be very cold.

—

Know how to answer hard or awkward interview questions. Know how to position yourself as the ideal candidate when you are over qualified? e.g., you want the job, and it doesn't bother you that you're over qualified, but the person hiring you may feel insecure in your capabilities compared to theirs.

—

How to develop your experience into valid examples and relate them back to any situation you could be asked in one of those 'tell me about a time when...' It's the learning / insight that I've found is often not addressed by interviewees.

—

Interviewees often focus on the task itself, rather than the key learning from the practical application / activity undertaken. Show me the insight, show me the value add you bring, not just a tick list of tasks.

—

Normally the interview is closed with do you have any questions for us?. If all your questions have coincidentally already been answered throughout the interview, know how to manage this question from the interviewer,

GETTING HIRED

without looking like you didn't have any prepared questions.

—

By the time you arrive at interview you will have passed through various screenings and therefore you are probably not trying to prove your skills & experience are valid contributions for the role. What you need to show above all is that you can work, get things done, indeed thrive within the work community.

The task you have is to show your personality in its best light. It's very hard and usually also very transparent to act an alternative character to who you really are so you need to, firstly know yourself and how others perceive you etc. and then build on this to show your best light.

—

You: articulate how you specific skills and experience can help them maintain and grow their business. Push your potential as well as established skills and experience. Be sure you know who you are and what you want. Be yourself and be personable. Them: This should mostly be about them and what they need (and how you fit) – you want to make it easy for them to slot you in – assume that you are in the job, what would be you plan. Questions: Ask a lot of questions – more listen than talk

—

Candidates should be succinct about how in the past they've accomplished the 3 or 4 goals set forth in the job description...be able to drill into the how and why they accomplished what they did.

—

For leadership and executive roles, accomplishments should including growing other leader capabilities, and improving team performance through restructuring, goals/metrics.

THOUGHTS AND SUGGESTIONS FROM COLLEAGUES

I think knowledge (via education & experience) related to the specific position in question is important.

—

I think to show/have an open, confident, and friendly personality will also gain others' trust and confidence.

—

Creating self-belief in the individual. They need to believe you are the right person for the role and approach the application with a winning attitude.

—

I have interviewed many candidates over the years. I usually can make up my mind in the first five minutes, is he/she a 'no,' or a 'maybe' or even possibly a 'yes.' The moral is that first impressions count - be ready.

—

If it is the first interview, the candidate should be 'selling.' The goal is to get offered the job. If it is a second interview, they are 'buying' and should be ready with questions, essentially to see if they want the job. I am very aware that good people have choices!

—

If the candidate has been out of work for a while, I am always interested in knowing what they did with the free time. Are they self-starters who have been productive or have they languished at home.

—

Age - for beyond entry-level jobs. To get any serious work experience, you need time, but the older you get, there is no excuse for not being successful.

—

Positivity! No whining about colleagues, projects, management, or previous positions. If a person complains during an interview, they will likely continue that behavior, and it can suck the life out of any team or project. I want someone who insists upon giving their current employer fair notice and respects their current employer's intellectual property. I once heard a manager brag about stealing a specifically formatted database from her former employer to use on an engagement.

—

Working is most commonly a community activity so that you can demonstrate that. Also, spending eight hours a day with you will not be a painful experience! Ask yourself, would I want to work with me, and why?

There is lots of research that shows people will choose/recruit candidates they like!

—

The candidate must demonstrate strategic acumen, to prove that they can go beyond performing tasks, but can choose which tasks should be performed, and what approach to the market, profits, customers, products, etc. should be pursued.

—

I think the biggest challenge of getting hired is convincing the hiring manager that you are the only candidate that could do the job and more! However, depending upon the position, you should promise just enough but not excessively more. Over promising may set up an unrealistic expectations with the hiring manager which could result in disappointment later.

Getting Hired

Show you have the cultural fit that is aligned to the organization. I mean the corporate culture, norms, and mores and being loyal to them - not just espousing them and not actively practicing them. If an organization wants to be innovative, diverse, inclusive, and bold, they are the cultural characteristics I hire for. If the interviewee can show me they fit this culture, then the skills can be taught afterward. Hire for cultural fit.

THOUGHTS AND SUGGESTIONS FROM COLLEAGUES

From my personal experience, we should focus on why first - why are my skills and experience the right fit for this job opportunity. As an interviewer, I rarely see folks that sell themselves to the job - they are more interested in what the job/company has for them. Sell yourself first to make sure the job is the right job for you, hen, the benefits, company culture, and other company-centric components will either make or break your decision to accept an offer.

—

How do you successfully negotiate parttime work? Work is a marathon and not a sprint, your working life is a 40-year marathon, so you need to know how to navigate parttime work and still be seen as the best candidate.

—

Best advice ever, sit in the lobby, car park, or coffee shop and watch these people you can work with or see you being part of!

—

As you become more senior, is this CEO someone you respect and the board you want to ultimately be accountable to? It's less about technical skills; it is about relationship and influence.

—

Negotiate terms, offer letters or employment contracts, including 1st-year goal expectations, and separation terms. I've seen people have an idea about the job, then after their hired and the annual goals are put together, it's a way different job.

—

Passion and understanding of the role and company/individual you are going to work with. Doing your homework is crucial and demonstrating that effort whenever the question allows you to show it. An absolute no for me is a candidate who wants to know the salary package at the first meeting.

161

GETTING HIRED

To negotiate one has to understand all the parts in the compensation package. The gross annual or monthly salary gives a good indication relative to the other offers; however there are other important parts beyond health insurance. The other parts can include sign-up bonuses, year-end performance bonuses, 401k matching, profit sharing, employee stock option grants (initial and annual), etc. I think this is more difficult for the younger, new employees to understand the potential value to the full extent.

—

For myself in biotech, I valued stock options and employee stock purchases. As an example, one of my former staff members was able to fortuitously boost her annual salary by 30% by selecting a particular stock purchase program. She was completely confused by the choices but followed the advice of a fellow employee who had also selected that particular program.

—

Luck: meeting the right people at the right time with the right job can be key – so step 1 is key so you have the best chance of timing it right

Online Resources

Your online resources are almost unlimited. By using Google search, you can answer nearly any question that you have. Rather than attempt to cover everything, I have listed some sites that may prove informative and helpful.

RECRUITING FIRMS

https://www.forbes.com/best-professional-recruiting-firms/

https://www.forbes.com/best-executive-recruiting-firms/

JOB SEARCH SITES

https://www.roberthalf.com/blog/job-market/10-best-job-search-websites

https://www.indeed.com

General Career Statistics and Information

https://www.bls.gov/ooh/

https://www.statista.com

PROJECT PLANNING AND MANAGEMENT

https://project-management.com/developing-the-project-management-plan/

https://www.pmi.org/pmbok-guide-standards

GENERAL

https://www.jamesclear.com

Note: For an updated list of consulting firms and accounting firms send a request to info@paulmcblaine.com.

GETTING HIRED

Your First Hundred Days Checklist

To get off to a great start in your new role, you need to hit the ground running. First impressions are critical, and the sooner you make a positive contribution, the better. This is a simple checklist for what you can do to jump-start your career during the first 100 days of a new job, a new role, or a new company. These items are not in order of importance or any sequential order, so review the whole list and scan it every day. At the beginning of each week, make a list of those items that you will complete during the week. Check this shortlist every day.

- Apply for business cards (if applicable).
- Attend employee orientation training or arrange for personal training.
- Keep a daily diary of activities, accomplishments, goals and to-do's.
- Carefully observe workflows and identify one opportunity to improve.
- Complete all assignments on time.
- Complete your W-4.
- Create a new short biography according to corporate guidelines.
- Create a list of your supervisor's specific goals for you for the first 100 days.
- Create your new Personal Marketing Message based on your new role.
- Determine who are the internal customers of your specific work products.
- Determine who you are your internal suppliers.
- Determine your Performance Review Schedule.

YOUR FIRST HUNDRED DAYS CHECKLIST

- Determine your work hours and any acceptable flexibility.
- Develop a training plan for yourself; include training for current role and future roles.
- Develop a training/learning plan for your first 90 days .
- Develop specific job goals - SMART - Specific, Measurable, Achievable, Relevant, Timely.
- Do something for the company that you identify needs to be done or fixed.
- Establish 401K contributions – if offered contribute at a level that gets the maximum company match.
- Familiarize yourself with the office/building layout.
- Familiarize yourself with your benefits.
- Find out about team meeting schedules - especially ones that you should participate in.
- Find out how you will be introduced to your team/department.
- Find out when there will be a company-wide internal announcement of your joining.
- Find out where to go and whom to talk with for help and assistance.
- Generate a list of specific deliverables with dates that they are due.
- Get access to corporate IT systems - i.e., log in details.
- Get an introduction to corporate IT systems (time reporting, data mining, analytics, etc.)
- Get assignments, work, projects, etc.
- Get involved in the general work of the company (beyond your role).
- Have someone explain the company history.
- Identify your workspace or how hoteling will work.

GETTING HIRED

- Interview representatives of your internal suppliers (people that you get work from) to help them understand your specific requirements.
- Interview representatives of your internal customers (people that you do work for) to understand their specific requirements.
- Introduce yourself to the administrative team and understand each of their roles.
- Meet with the supervisor's boss to introduce yourself.
- Meet with your co-workers to get to know them.
- Meet with your supervisor to build rapport and understand her/his requirements.
- Obtain a copy of the job requirements for your next career step.
- Obtain an official copy of your job description and job responsibilities.
- Obtain a current organization chart.
- Obtain and set up your laptop (if applicable).
- Obtain a copy of the corporate strategic plan if possible.
- Obtain a copy of the corporate Mission, Vision, Values.
- Obtain necessary office supplies.
- Obtain your security clearance and badge..
- Obtain your supervisor's approval of your specific job goals.
- Outline your personal career goals for the first 100 days.
- Get invited and participate in meetings – participation and contribution are essential.
- Read and carefully understand your job description and duties.
- Make a list for each item in #49 and how you will achieve each item.

YOUR FIRST HUNDRED DAYS CHECKLIST

- Request a buddy - someone at your level, who has been in the company for more than one year.
- Request a mentor - a senior person who is not in your chain of command.
- Request to connect with all of your new colleagues on LinkedIn.
- Research the industry you are now in and become an expert in one small thing.
- Review and understand your Performance Review Criteria.
- Review the external announcement of your joining (if appropriate).
- Review your new job description with your supervisor, clarify expectations and establish priorities.
- Review your specific job goals with your supervisor.
- Schedule a weekly update with the supervisor.
- Schedule brief meetings with the executive team to introduce yourself.
- Select one idea from your list of ideas and discuss with your supervisor.
- Send out a notice of your new position to all of your contacts and your original email and new phone number.
- Set up your email account.
- Share one piece of knowledge from past jobs or roles with your team.
- Start a list of ideas to add value to the company.
- Understand business as usual.
- Understand expense tracking rules.
- Understand the payroll schedule and processes.
- Understand performance review process deadlines.

GETTING HIRED

- Understand the roles of all of your colleagues and co-workers.
- Understand timekeeping rules.
- Understand what it takes to exceed performance expectations in your first three months.
- Arrive on-time or early and leave after your boss.
- Answer all emails, texts, phone calls (immediately if possible or one hour if in meetings).
- Understand and develop a simple plan for your next career step(s).
- Update your LinkedIn profile.
- Update your resume.
- Volunteer for internal initiatives (writing white paper or research).
- Write a personal email to everyone in your network about your new role.
- Thank everyone who helped you get the role.
- Find someone on your new team to help.

NOTE: To receive an electronic copy of "Your first hundred days" checklist send your request to info@paulmcblaine.com.

Acknowledgements

I would like to thank all of my friends, colleagues, and clients who were kind enough take the time to give me their ideas, comments, criticism, and thoughts that helped me make this book better. Their intellectual insights, wisdom gained through their impressive careers, and willing generosity humble me. I surveyed all of them and incorporated their thoughts and ideas.

James Alt-Graham, Max Abraham, James Bill, Robin Boyer, Bruce Dick, Dan Gee, Gayle Golden, Linda Justin, Liz Koh, Wayne Little, Bill McEleney, Glen Mannering, Mahsa Merat, David Ockleshaw, Brenden Polsen, Dhwani Patel, Lili Parsai, Laurance Reed, Martin Radvan, Mike Rae, Alicia Simons, Mike Sonne, Lisa Thakur, Brad Wurm, David Wilk, Thong Way

About the Author

Paul McBlaine was born in Champaign, Illinois. Paul's life changed forever when his father accepted a job in California working with the first computers. His family bravely undertook the cross-country road trip to California along Route 66, with three children under 12. His wanderlust was born on that summer trip.

He grew up in the town of Corona, 60 miles east of Los Angeles. After high school, he joined the Navy and was trained to repair cryptographic equipment. He was stationed in San Diego, San Francisco, Norfolk, VA, Morocco, and Japan and made side trips to Europe and the Philippines.

He was a voracious reader of English literature and was inspired to write. He kept extensive journals of his world travels, wrote poetry and short stories. The results is stacks of work are still waiting to be published.

Returning home, he earned Masters in Biochemistry and Biology before landing his first industry position at Baxter Biotech as a researcher. While pursuing his MBA, he wrote his first paper on the importance of career development and owning your career.

True to his thesis, Paul pivoted his career more than twenty times over the next four decades. As a management consultant, he worked in the U.S., Australia, and London in multiple industries where he coached and mentored hundreds of individuals helping them further their careers.

Paul and his wife Lili, make their home in Chicago, where he is the fourth generation to live, work and play.

REVIEW ASK

LOVE THIS BOOK? DON'T FORGET

TO LEAVE A REVIEW!

EVERY REVIEW MATTERS, AND IT MATTERS A LOT!

PLEASE HEAD OVER TO AMAZON OR WHEREVER YOU PURCHASED THIS BOOK TO LEAVE AN HONEST REVIEW FOR ME.

I THANK YOU ENDLESSLY.

***

WANT TO READ MORE?

Watch for new titles in

SERIES

COMING IN 2021:

BEING A CONSULTANT

A Complete Guide To a Career as a Consultant

WWW.PAULMCBLAINE.COM

www.ingramcontent.com/pod-product-compliance
Lightning Source LLC
Chambersburg PA
CBHW021858230426
43671CB00006B/438